Traditional Religious Systems of the Rengma Nagas

Traditional Religious Systems of the Rengma Nagas

Kenilo Kath

Maulana Abul Kalam Azad Institute of Asian Studies, Kolkata

ANSHAH Anshah Publishing House

The views expressed in the study are those be of the author and not of the Maulana Abul Kalam Azad Institute of Asian Studies, Kolkata, and the author is solely responsible for the content.

ISBN: 81-8364-003-6

First Published in India in 2005

Traditional Religious Systems of the Rengma Nagas

Published by:
ANSHAH PUBLISHING HOUSE
H4-03, Mayurdhwaj, 60 I P Extention
Delhi-110092, INDIA
Phone: 9213355060, 9213387134

Preface

History of the Nagas is shrouded in obscurity, more so in respect of the origin and migration because there is no written accounts. This makes it extremely difficult to write any history of the origin and migration of the Nagas in general and the Rengma Nagas in particular. However an effort is made to study the Traditional Religious System of the Rengma Nagas and the impact of Christianity during 1824-1972.

I am thankful to Prof. Mahavir Singh, Director, Maulana Abul Kalam Azad Institute of Asian Studies, Kolkata for extending support and cooperation to make the study possible.

Kenilo Kath

Contents

Chapter 1

Origin, Migration and Dispersal

The Naga tribes inhabit the hills south-east of Assam dividing that province from the north-west portion of Burma. That large extent of mountainous country is bounded on the west by the Kopili river and the east frontier of Tipperrah in nearly East longitude 93° on the east and south-east by the hills dividing Assam from the Bor-khamti country in Longitude 97° and the valley of the Kyendrens.[1]. In the north the valley of Assam, and by the Patkoi hill ranges 27°2'10" North latitude and in the south by an imaginary line, nearly corresponding with the 23 degree of North latitude is inhabited by numerous tribes of highlanders known to the Assamese, Bengalese and Manipuris by the general name of the Nagas, and to Burma by the term of Kekhyens

History of the Nagas is shrouded in obscurity, more so in respect of the origin and migration because there is no written accounts. This makes it extremely difficult to write any history of the origin and migration of the Nagas in general and the Rengma Nagas in particular. However, we have endeavoured to make an effort on the basis of written and oral tradition.

Origin of the Word 'Naga'

The origin of the name 'Naga' has given rise to some considerable speculation with the result that there are several theories in existence each with some foundation but with no unanimity of opinion. This term 'Nagas' includes the various tribes of the present state of Nagaland, the tribes Nocte, Wancho, Tangsa, etc. of North-East Frontier Agency and their congeners in Manipur State in Sumra tract of Burma[2]. Many think that the Naga (after Assamese Nanga)[3] means Naked; sometimes it is suggested that the word means a snake probably connected with Naga snake charmers of the Aryan history. It is also surmised that it is a nickname used by plain men for a Hillman on the contention that the so-called backward hill tribes of central India are called Naga by the Hindus.[4]

According to the European scholars such as Gait, Peal, Holcombe, Elwin, etc. the word Naga is derived from some of the tribal dialects 'Nok', which means 'folks'. According to Mawu Gwizan, the term is derived from the Chinese word Natcha because the Chinese call the Nagas Natcharemi meaning 'Naga People'. Another view which had been widely accepted about the origin of the term Naga is derived from the Burmese word 'Noka' meaning perforated ears.

The origin of the word Naga is unknown; but it has been supposed by some to have been derived from the Sanskrit word and applied in derision to the people for the paucity of their clothing; but there seems little foundation for this etymological derivation, as the term has never been known to be applied by the Bengalese to either the Khasias or Garos with whom they were far better acquainted than with the Nagas; and besides the Garos especially are habitually accustomed to a greater degree of nudity than any of the Naga tribes with whom we are acquainted.[5] Whatever be the origin of the word Naga, not one of these derivations is satisfactory nor does it really concern us much to know about it, seeing that the name is quite foreign to and unrecognised by the Naga themselves. They have no generic term for the whole race or even for each of the various tribes contributing the race[6]. The inhabitants of these hills are divided into numerous communities or races and they know themselves by the designation of their respective tribes only and not by the name common to all the races.

There, however, appears to be some mark by which these tribes are distinguished from their neighbours and some common ties by which they are all bound together as one people, though possibly at present divided into tribes by a diversity of dialect. In all probability, this common tie may have descended to all the present tribes from the great aboriginal stock by which the hills were first peopled. Other races may from time to time have entered and taken refuge in the hills, bringing with them their own dialects; but they may have probably amalgamated with the old stock in habits and manners, and above all in religious superstitions; and these last especially may form the great connecting link of all the Nagas and the cause of separation from other hill tribe.

The origin of the word 'Rengma' is unknown to the Rengmas. Originally, the Southern and the Western Rengmas called themselves Nzonyu, the Northern Rengmas and the Eastern Rengmas called themselves Nthini. The 'term Rengma' has a number of interpretations. The first theory is that the Kheza people called them Remami, which later came to be known as Rengma. It is believed that the Rengma were the first people to split from the other Naga brothers from the Khezakenoma, the last common Naga Village; and they moved Westward and established a new village near present Kegwema village. From then, the people of Khezha called them as Renmami, which is derived from the 'Re' meaning 'village' and 'ma' meaning 'to have missed', and thereby implying people who missed their village. The other interpretation is that when the English saw 'Nzonyu' in thick forest of Assam, near Mohang – Deboa (present Depoka area); they were found wearing full brass rings, earrings, bangles, necklace etc. Hence, the English called these people as 'Ringman'. With the passage of time, the Ringman was anglicised into Rengma and therefore, the Nzanyu has come to be known as Rengma.

History bears testimony to the fact that the Rengma Nagas were already living in the plains of Assam generations before the Burmese army invaded Assam, culminating in the loss of her independence and ultimately yielding to the treaty of Yandabo in 1826. In this invasion, Keyhon the warrior fought alongside the Ahom Kings with his comrades in arms. The defeat of the invading Burmese army was largely due to the relentless resistance and stubborn fight put up by Keyhon and his men, and in recognition of his heroic actions in the defence of the country and for rendering distinguished service of the highest order, Keyhon was conferred the title of Phookan. The story of Keyhon Phookan's encounter with a high British official goes that when the latter wanted to see the Ahom King, the king did not want to see the British official himself; and so he asked the courtiers to send someone else on his behalf. Keyhon got himself dressed up in his traditional warriors' apparel and went to see the British official. When the British official saw him coming, he was dumbfounded by the spectacle of a strange apparition clad in grotesque clothes. The British official asked Keyhon Phookan through an interpreter what was called in Keyhon's language the ghostly appearance, which frightened people when one was asleep. Keyhon gave the ghosts name (nightmare) as 'Rema'. Later when Keyhon was leaving after his meeting, he heard the Britishers referring to him as 'Rema' 'Rima' and

'Rengma' and finally the term Rengma was applied to his tribe too.[7]

But his interpretation is not much acceptable to some historians. John Butler's record *Travel in Assam*, mention that "In 1839, Mr. Grange, Sub-Assistant Commissioner seems to have been the first European officer who met the Rengma Nagas in the vicinity of Mohang Dijon on his way to the Angami hills".[8] Mr. Grange has mentioned nothing about the word 'Rengma' in his account on the Rengma Nagas.

Theories of Migration

The Nagas who settled in the Naga Hills have various theories about their migration, often recorded by the foreign writers. However, the earliest specific reference to the Nagas was made by Claudius Ptolemy in 150 A.D. in his *geographia* where he referred to the Naga country as the "The Realm of the Naked".[9]

On the basis of language, their origin is assigned by Sir G.A. Grierson to that of the Tibeto — Burmese, who came with the second wave of migration from north of the Yangtse-Kiang and Hoang-Ho rivers[10]. Huang-Tsang, The Chinese pilgrim who visited Assam during Bhaskar Varman's rule in 645 A.D. said, "The east of this country is bounded by a line of hills, so that there is no great city to the kingdom. The frontiers are contiguous to the barbarians of South-West China. These tribes are in fact akin to those of the man people in their customs[11]." Ahom Buranjees also recorded that by the time the Ahoms came to Assam in the thirteenth century, Nagas were already settled in their present homeland. They wrote of the Nagas' resistance to Sukhapa, the founder of the Ahom Kingdom. However, from all these pieces of evidence, the exact date of the arrival of the Nagas cannot be established with precision, but at the same time, the fact that they have settled in their present homeland for many centuries cannot be ruled out.

A tradition in vogue amongst the Angamis, the Rengma, the Lothas and the Semas is that their forefathers came together in one migration and reached their present abode via Manipur and Burma.

It is said that when the Rengmas were on their way along with other tribes to Kezhakenoma, en-route via Manipur, a fierce tiger was in wait at some mountain precipice and mowing down all the people passing through. A warrior by name 'Kerhe' had devised the means of breaking the reeds to see whether the tiger was in deep sleep and seeing the tiger in sleep, he speared the tiger to death which allowed their escape from the mouth of the tiger. They, with the Lothas, Semas and the Angamis, have settled at Kezhakenoma but how long they lived together was not recorded or conveyed by the tale. They must have spent their time together at least some years, because they relate the story of the khezhakenoma magic stone as well as many other folktales common to the Angami, Lotha and Sema. They, with the Lothas, the Angamis and the Semas, belong to the group of tribes that placed their point of dispersal at khezhakenoma, due east of Mao.

As with the other tribes, the cause of the dispersal is said to have been a dispute over the stone, which had the miraculous power of increasing rice dried on it[12]. If one load of rice was dried on this, it became two loads. There was, the story goes, once upon a time an old couple with three sons living in that village. Every day they used to spread paddy to dry upon a great flat stone, and by dusk, a single load spread to dry had become two loads, for the stone was inhabited by a spirit. The three sons used to take turns to spread their paddy on this stone, but one day they quarrelled bitterly as to whose turn it was, and their parents, fearing bloodshed, broke an egg on the stone, covered it with brushwood, laid faggots around it and set the whole on fire. The stone burst with a crack like thunder, the spirit went up to heaven in a cloud of smoke and the virtue of the stone departed[13]. According to the Lotha tradition, in order to put an end to the quarrels of the brothers as to whose turn it was to dry and double his paddy, an old man, who had no wife, and an old woman, who had no husband, were selected and these two had sexual connection lying on the stone. This destroyed the miraculous properties. Possibly the idea was that the sexual act between those old people was bound to be sterile and that this sterility should be communicated to the highly prolific stone. Owing, however, to the indecent behaviour of a man of the tribe, the virtue went out of the stone, and the Lothas set out on their migrations, taking with them a piece of the stone. This is still preserved at Pangti.

It was here that the Rengmas split to migrate in different directions like those of Angami, Lotha and Sema. According to Rengma tradition, the first recorded settlement of the individual body of migrants was at the present Angami Village of Kegwima (Kagwenyu). And from here, the first division among the Rengma migrants took place. A group of people went towards the present Khonoma village and settled there for some few years, but neither the name nor exact site is known. At Khonoma a man named Keviso had two sons, Marasa and Khaki. Marasa happened to be a very smart and good sports person. Every year he won the games played during the festivals. People became jealous of him and planned a plot to kill him, but his girlfriend came to know of the conspiracy and informed him. He then left the village and proceeded northwards to Nerhema. Marasa got a son named Pesosü who later on left his birthplace[14] and went northern side where he joined his Rengma brothers at Kwemphang[15].

The larger group moved to Chedema (below Kohima Village), and from Chedema they went to Khwemphe (Ngachügi) via Thizama, Nbajan (Nerhema), Nashanyu (Karphema). It was from here the major split of the Rengmas took place. A section of people went north, keeping down the slope of the high ridge, and founded Tsegwenyu Phang (present N.A.P Camp). The ancestors of the Lothas and Semas were still with them, and the Monoliths set up by the former can be seen to this day. It was here that the ancestors of the Semas split off. The rest of Tsegwenyu Phang, which still included the ancestors of the Lothas, went on north to Aghonshü, a site to the east of Tesophenyu. From here the Lothas split off and set out for their present country, first leaving their valuable loads buried in pots, with the seed of a big tree in each pot which would grow up and mark the spot[16]. The Rengmas too, abandoned Aghonshü and split. One group moved up to the upper sections of Tesophenyu which is the largest village in Rengma, and another body went north and founded Khitagha (Nsunyu), group the last went to the most northerly part of the tribe and established Kandinu village called after Kandi name who chose the areas and performed the religious rites. Exact spot and time could not be traced[17], however, according to the tradition; the Eastern Rengmas had migrated from this group to the eastern part of Nagaland and formed three villages, Sahunu, Meluri and Lephori, on the Burma side of the Barrel watershed. It is said, a white stag came to their village, and a group of men went chasing the stag. "... They followed the deer so far that they lost their way, so they settled on their present site...."[18] where rice and rice beer and the earthen pot comes out of the *bambusa* and the earth they cut and dug respectively. The animal always kept close to them while hunting till dusk, and when they woke up in the morning they found the stag standing near them. In such a way they took some days to hunt the animal, until they reached a wonderful site where they received rice, rice beer and the earthen pot from the spirit God. There, they established a village Epunu. They were being forced to move eastward, as the Semas and the Angamis were moving behind them. They settled at Mutsalu and then proceeded to Ketsabu (kitsaben). The Eastern Angamis' raid drove them to the Tizu valley from where they split into three groups. One group moved north and founded Suhunu village at the bank of the river. The other two groups moved east and formed Milomi (Meluri) village and Mipfuri (Lephori) village with about twenty kilometers distance between them.

The distance between the two kinsmen was too far to travel by foot, and in between the Semas and the Eastern Angamis (Chakesang) had fenced their contact. Besides, it became taboo to visit each other, because when they visited each other and shared their sorrows and longing, the guests after reaching their village did not live long and die. We can see J.P. Mills' Tour Diary account, "I have with me Putho, the leading man of Milori (Naked Rengma) and four attendants. It is strictly speaking *genna* for naked Rengma to visit other Rengma country, and none of them have ever done so". But they say it is not *genna* if I take them, and they are very keen to see the villages from which their ancestors came an unknown number of generations ago. The meeting between the Melori men and their kinsmen was really most impressive. An old man made an impromptu and impassioned speech of welcome and both sides were soon busy comparing traditions of the split many, many generations ago, old men estimated sixteenth generation."[19]. It is worth quoting Mills narration of an enormous deputation awaited them below Therugu Hill, where the forefathers of the tribes had once lived. An old man addressed them and said, "Welcome, you are our brethren. We are of one stock. We know that you left us long ago, but the fields, the rocks and the trees of our land are still yours as well as ours. It is only because you live so far away that you cannot use them. Eat with us and drink with us now, and when you return to your country, go in peace."[20]

It is improper without dealing with the Southern and Western migrants from the major split site. Tsemi along with his people from the Khwenphang moved north and founded Tseminyu village named after him. Another body moved west and founded Sendenyu village named after Senden who led the party. After some years Thongsu, the younger brother of Senden, founded a new village Thongsünyu[21] named after him. Thongsü had seven good warriors[22] who defend the pressure of the Angamis. But one day, while going to attack the enemy, on the way all of them suddenly disappeared[23]. The village could no longer withstand the enemies' raids, they were compelled to move north. With the disappearance of Thongsünyu village, Sendenyu could no longer resist the harassment of enemies as well as witchcraft and as a result a large group of people moved to west to the plains of Assam. It is said that in those days, Sendenyu was the most populated village of the tribe. In a day, a whetstone kept on the main field path used to finish by the people going to field. When the children were sent to fetch water, firewood etc, most of the time, they returned empty handed. Life for the old men and women became not easy to survive. Hence, one day, Mr. Peno had decided to depopulate the village by witch. He went down to Chungsanyu village to meet his friend who knew the method to kill the people without war. When he narrated the whole matter to his excited host friend, the latter instead of agreeing with the former scolded him and advised him to give up the plot. In the morning, knowing the evil plan of his friend, he insisted his friend go back home and left for the field. But Peno refused to go without knowing the method, and stayed for three days, till he succeeded in his mission. On the third night, though he was angry but could not withstand the pressure of Peno and he was compelled to teach him, but not without condition he taught him[24]. He said, "It is a sin and I am not responsible for this cause". When he came back to the village and did it as he learned from his friend, the result was that the villagers were tired of burying the dead bodies. The population declined to a minimum number, thereby a large number of people moved downward to the west by saying, "the stone too, rolled down, the trees too, fell downside". These people crossed the plains of Dimapur, and marched to settle at the present site called the Rengma Hills.

It was clear that some group from Khwenphang must split. So, they began to move off and found villages at the top of Terügu hill and Kashanyu. The village at Terüguthong was too windy; every year the village got burned down. Besides, scarcity of water and clouds in the winter season made harsh living conditions. In due course of time this group of people moved to the present Rengma Hills led by some leaders Kheno, Shonphu and Keto about 16 generations ago. This section was considered as the first migrants to the plains of Assam. They migrated slowly to the hill region.

Another phase of migration from Kashanyu to the present Rengma Hills of Assam was much talked about. According to the tradition there lived a great warrior by the name Nzondegibu, born and brought up at Kashanyu village. He was not only a brave warrior, but a wise and intelligent young man whose ambition was to expand the territory of the Rengmas. He left his native village and went to settle at the Sendenyu village; there he was admired by young and old. For fear of the enemies' raid in their absence, the parents keep their children under the care of the great warrior Nzondigibu whenever they went to the field. In order to fulfill his ambition he used to train the young boys how to handle dao, spear and shield to fight in the war, while all the men and women were busy working in their field. He used to butcher villagers' pigs and cocks and feed the boys in their absence. One-day, when the trained young boys who became fit to handle the weapons, he organized a great feast for them by killing the village pigs, cocks, cows etc. After a great feast, he convinced them to go for war, and requested them to get ready for a march. The wise warrior arranged food stuff for some days and led them towards the west carrying all their needs for some days. When the villagers returned from the field, they were shocked to see their village without the hero and their young boys.

Nobody knows in which direction this party left. Helpless villagers searched for them for some days without hope. Nzondigubu, with his men established the first village Tsokudunyu some kilometers below the present Tsosinyu village. Several times he had visited the kingdom of Duma Raja (King of Demahpoor)[25] collecting food items and weapons. As he becomes a frequent visitor to the King's place, the queen fell in love with him. The king became suspicious of the two. So one day he fooled his wife telling her that he was going for hunting, but returned halfway. When he came back, he found the queen and Tegibu sitting inside the queen's chamber. Tegibu was arrested and put in the lion's cage by the king. But the queen secretly told him the method to escape from the lion's mouth. "You will be taken to darbar hall where you will be allowed to choose from the swords kept in large numbers. You have to choose the rusted one." Secondly she secretly gave him a piece of animal skin and said, "When you enter the cage, the lion will roar like thunder three times. It will look as if it is about to swallow at first and after second roar the lion will go back but after the third it will jump at you and swallow you. So put the skin inside the mouth at the third roar and kill the lion with the sword." He did what the queen advised him to do and was miraculously saved from the mouth of the lion. After killing the lion, he jumped over the fifteen foot high wall shouting a war cry and challenging the Raja. The Raja replied, "Oh Tegibu! You are also a man." and then set him free. For many days, Tegibu tried to enter the king's place, but he failed. One day he got the chance to enter while the king was out of station. Tegibu asked the queen how to kill the king. She replied, "Most of the days, he used to take bath in the midst of the day. You can attempt his life at this time." Tegibu tried several times, but it was a failure. However, one day, he got the chance to climb over the wall and directly enter the lake where the king was bathing. He went near him and said, "Raja, if you are a man come here. Unless you come here, I will not leave you." Shocked, the king could only swim around the pool till he became tired and cold. Then Tegibu killed the king and became the king of Dimapur. But his kingship could not last long due to his ignorance and disobedience. The father of the queen, hearing the tragic news was affronted and with great anger he cursed the new couple and restricted them from coming to his house. It so happened that one day, while the king was returning from hunting, he felt thirsty. The young Raja, unable to control his thirst, went inside his father-in-law's house, which was on his way, and quenched his thirst. The Raja then fell sick with a swollen body for some days and died. The death of the Rengma Raja of Demaphpoor compelled the Rengmas to further migrate west until they reached the present settled Rengma Hills.

How far it is true? None of the historians has yet discovered the facts of the western Rengma migrants to their present abode due to non-availability of the written record, but, we cannot deny the fact that once upon a time some sections had split off from their proper Rengma. Therefore, the above oral traditions recovered in recent years talk about their migration, which cannot be simply denied.

The Rengma Nagas, who have been living in the Rengma Hills, were the first among the Rengmas to encounter with the European Mr. Grange (then sub-Assistant Commissioner of Nowgong district) in the vicinity of Mohung Dehoon on his way to the Angami Hills in 1839. Thereafter, they took the help of the Rengmas for further exploration. Thus the entire homeland of the Rengmas in Assam lying between Bora Dikharu Nallah, on the north, The Jemuna River and Diphu River in the south, course of Bora Dikharu and Hora Dikharu in the west and in the east including Dimapur was declared and constituted as the Rengma Hills with its headquarters at Samaguting in 1866. "I have marked this boundary with blue crosses as far as the Rengma Naga, and with red and blue crosses on to the Doyang"[26]. It was only in 1847, Captain Butler, Principal Assistant, induced several of the most influential chiefs to visit Nowgong, on which occasion they readily assented to be taxed one Rupee per house, and gave him a written agreement to that effect. This measure being approved by the Agent to the Governor-General, Mr. Sub-Assistant Master was deputed in December, 1847, to enter Rengma Hills from Golaghaut; but after visiting many villages, that gentleman found the country so heavy and impassable due to the dense wet jungles that he was constrained to return to the plains at Kageerunga. He again met with the Rengma Nagahs on his route over the Meekir via Bannenee, Sildhampur, on the Mohung Dehooa; when the first revenue settlement with all the Rengma Naga villages, discovered — thirty-two in number, was successfully accomplished[27].

The other groups of the Rengmas such as Northern and Southern Rengmas who are the parent bodies, came in contact with the Europeans John Butler and Dr. Brown W.F.

Badgley in 1872 and the Eastern Rengma in 1874 respectively. Proper Rengmas today, as we may call, are found to inhabit the land surrounded by Angamis in the south, the Lothas in the north and the Semas in the east, but a group long ago went and ensconced in the Eastern Chakesang extremities while a group was diverted to Borporthar area in the outlying plains.[28]

Notes and References

1. William Robinson, *A Descriptive Account of Assam* 1841, p. 380.
2. *A Brief Historical Account of Nagaland*, Naga institute of Culture, Kohima, p. 21.
3. *A Corruption of Sanskrit*. (Gazetteer of India).
4. *Gazetteer of India*, Nagaland; Kohima District. 1970, p. 10.
5. William Robinson, *A Descriptive Account of Assam* 1841, pp. 80.
6. Verrier Elwin, *The Nagas in the 19th Century* 1969, p. 47.
7. G.K. Ghosh, *Tribal and Their Culture*, Manipur & Nagaland. Vol. 3, p. 7.
8. John Butler; *Travels in Assam*. P
9. Claudius Ptolemy; *Geographic VII* i.e. p. 18.
10. Grierson G.A., *Linguistic Survey of India*, Vol. III, Part II, Varanasi, 1903; p. 11.
11. Thomas Watters, *On Chwang's Travels in India*, (A.D. 625-645), London, 1904 Delhi. Reprint 1973, p. 186.
12. Vide The Sema Naga, p. 5; *The Angami Naga*, p. 19; The Lotha Nagas, p. 3.
13. *The Angami Nagas*, p. 19
14. Probably after his father's death.
15. An Oral Interview with Homa Thong of Sendenyu Village.
16. J.P. Mills, *The Rengma Nagas*, p. 6.
17. According to J.P. Mills, Khitagha. Where as another tradition said it is from Kandinu. The name of a person inukandi who still live at Suhunu village is the tenth named after their ancestor's name Kandi who established the Kandinu village. Nurhitho,

Nyutomerhri and Saphe were the people returned home to call their wives and children and then went back to their new village.

18. Tour Diary of Captain A.E. Woods, I.S.C. Deputy Commissioner Naga Hills, 1930
19. Deputy Commissioner Naga Hills, 1930.
20. J.P. Mills, *The Rengma Nagas*, p. 8.
21. Present Government High School, Sendenyu.
22. Only five names could be recollected: Makhunthon. Keyhon, Kelera, Katheshen, Ashantu, Renzu.
23. It was believed that they might have turned to spirits.
24. Chanu (broom leaf), nchu, hair, shaving blade, ncho, gvürü and etc. were wrapped and dug in the main field path. Whoever stepped on it died?
25. J. Butler's record, Reign of Chukurdog, Rajah of Assam, who died in 1663
26. Brief Memorandum on the Naga country by John Butler, 1873. Enclosed several maps of India's Frontiers.
27. A.J. Moffat Mills, Report on Assam. Esq., Gyan Publications, Delhi.
28. Gazetteer of India, Nagaland, Kohima district.

Chapter 2

Ancestors' Religion

The religion of the Rengmas is of that type which is conveniently termed 'Animism'. In the language of philosophy, Animism is the doctrine, which places the source of mental and even physical life in energy independent of or at least distinct from the body. From the point of view of the body of Rengma religion, the term is taken in a wider sense, to denote the belief in the existence of spiritual being, some attached to bodies of which they constitute the real personality (soul), and others without necessary connexion with a determinate body (spirits). James Hastings in his book *Religion and Ethics* said, "Animism in the sense just stated represents an attempt to explain in a rational way all the facts of the universe. It is the religion and the philosophy of all none-civilized peoples. It predominates the commencement of all the historical forms of worship. Finally, it still shows itself in its complete development in the survival of folk-lore". Tylor wrote in his great work *Primitive Culture* (1871) that animism is the attribution of a soul or spirit to living things and inanimate objects. In full-blown animism, nothing is really inanimate; everything is alive with spirit, alive or not. Further, Tylor felt that religion had its origin in early man's attribution of a soul like his own to every sort of living being and physical objects around him. Religion is a man's establishment of relationship between himself and the spirit, which felt, possessed, pervaded, and crowded all nature. But Sir James Frazer, in *The Golden Bough*, lays down that when definite deities with specific names and functions are recognized, the animist has become a Polytheist, and the term 'Animism' is no longer strictly applicable.

Like the other hill tribes, Rengmas acknowledge the power of a plurality of spirits; and sacrifices of cows, pigs and fowls are offered on all occasions. The Rengma's idea of the deities and spirits in which he believes is so vague that he never even attempts to reproduce in pictures or carvings the mental image which he may form of them in his mind[1]. He is, however, definite about the kinds of offerings that should be given to the spirits at particular ceremonies.

Who are the spirits? Is there any Supreme Being worshipped by the Rengmas? This has to be studied in wider sense before describing their mode of worship. Though there is no written scripture, yet, their ideas of God and faith in the Supreme Being are well expressed in their traditional songs, myths, folktales, names, and other traditions. The people perceived their Supreme Lord as Aniza or Sungigü; Spirit God, who dwells in heaven and regarded as the creator, sustainer, and dispenser of the whole Universe. It is said, God lives with asükhi who bore the misery of the world. One day God asked him to create the earth. Accordingly he created the earth so plain; looking at the work of asükhi, God did not like it, He then reshaped the earth into spherical, having mountains, rivers, plains as well. Asükhi lived under the supervision of God. One day, God sent him to the earth and gave him the power to rule over the beasts, fowls and sea creatures. People believed him as the spirit of wealth, who is partial in distribution of blessings. They said Asükhi gives many blessings (in terms of wealth) to a section of people only and gives little or nothing to the remaining people, whereas God shares equal to all. They literally considered *Asükhi* as the god of wealth and thereby propitiate her by offering sacrifices and other means of worship. Whereas in their prayers of seeking blessing they always addressed Asükhi-Niza = Asukhi-God, sometimes when they received a good amount of paddy in harvest or other things they say asükhi-Niza has given.

When they celebrate thanksgiving ceremonies or festivals; they appease God for favour by offering meat, beer and other means of merry making, such as dancing and singing[2]. Here, in their prayers, they address the spirit God. Their ideas of Supreme Lord, however, are not faint and confused. He lives very far high and does not interfere in the day to day behavior of human-beings[3]. He is supreme and benevolent which is thought to be the guardian of the welfare and prosperity of human beings. Likewise Asükhi-Niza or Sunpri is considered as benevolent spirit but may get angry sometimes[4]. In this regard, their mode of worshipping God was the same, as the Christian belief in Holy Trinity; Father, Son and Holy Spirit.

Whatever may be their belief in God or a future state, it is certain that they believed in infinity of evil spirits or demons. Like the English words satan, demon, evil etc. the Rengmas used atsonghan, gijon, ayenya, miya-miya, axhashon, ghasipfü, kemichu etc.[5] Out of it, atsonghan is considered as the chief of evil spirits who cause death, sickness, natural calamities which brings hardship to human life, and to malevolent interference are ascribed all the woes which afflict mankind. To him, therefore, sacrifices must be offered. These malevolent spirits are Sylvan deities, spirits of trees, the rocks and the streams and sometimes also souls of the tribal ancestors.[6]

Malevolent spirits are sometimes chased away by burning leaves. It was believed that the Satan goes away on inhaling the smell of the burning leaves. The spirit called Ayenya can be heard talking like a man and calling out peoples' names. However, when one goes to where the sound comes from, there is nothing. It is very unlucky indeed to hear one's name being called by one of these spirits. Another very similar term called Remme or Ayen, appears at night when one is asleep. To them is attributed that very unpleasant type of nightmare in which one feels one cannot move. It is believed that when a man has one of these dreams, an evil spirit is lying on top of him, and would hold him down and suffocate him. Were it not that, these spirits are like men, but not quite complete. The Southern group of Western Rengmas says that each one lacks a thumb, and so cannot throttle a man. Other Rengmas say that they have no big toes, and so cannot hold still the big toes of the man they attack. A man fighting one, therefore, always tries to move his big toes, and if he succeeds in doing so, he knows he will get free[7]. If a man suffers frequently from nightmares of this kind, he puts up a slat of tsomho wood (tsomoho kesho – 'tsomho slat'. A. Azang satsatsetsü – "Azang frightener" – B. by his door, with tiger's eyes or rough human figures drawn on with charcoal.[8]

The spirits most in touch with man are spirits of earth, which they inhabit. The true earth spirits of the occultists, often deliberately harmful, are beneficent only when propitiated, though there is perhaps a tendency for purely maleficent spirits to take on, as a result of the habit of propitiation, the attributes of beneficent deities. There are several Naga traditions of little wild men or spirits of the woods having been found and caught and tamed[9]. In any case, the ayenya include the spirits of the forest, who are often heard, though not seen. There are spirits attached to individuals and houses, and perhaps villages, though it is difficult to obtain a precise description and probably no very definite conception.[10]

One kind called *tetse*; *miya-miya*, are more kindly spirits numbering ten or more. They lead people away into the jungle by singing folk songs in full harmony and shouting, a notion which may have something to do with the incessant 'ho-ho' -kept up by a Rengma working or carrying a load. Without its full number, it cannot lead away people, even if made temporarily mad. "miya-miya" makes a man do all sorts of unpleasant things – eat worms, for instance, make and wear a necklace of huge worms, or put them in his ears. He makes a man think the level ground the brink of a precipice and go hesitatingly in fear lest he fell over; or again a cliff appears level ground so that he runs up it, or falls over it. These spirits still prevail in our area.

All Nagas believe that one of the commonest causes of illness is theft of the soul by an evil spirit. Among the Rengmas these are called Atsonghang or Aring. They live in 'bad places' and heavy jungle, and sometimes appear as a gleaming red cock or a snake, and then disappear. When seen the people will fall sick[11]. They leave the chicken in the jungle and call the soul of the sick, or sacrifice the cock at home to propitiate the spirits to leave the soul of the sick. When this is done, the sick man becomes well. (Chickens freed and driven away in the jungle to serve as a substitute for the person turning them out or perhaps merely as an offering for the spirits of the jungle, or, it may be, to carry away the element of sickness or misfortune that attaches to the person who devote them to this purpose) are called chisu and regarded as accursed. A particularly evil one lives in a pool below Tseminyu which is believed to be bottomless. The pool is called Tihatsü lo zu (Tihatsü's field water). Tihatsü was a woman who struck the ground with her hoe and caused water to gush out, making a noise like 'tsü, tsü', part of her name. To see the spirit means serious illness and probably death. Ransoms for the souls spirits have caught are left by the paths, or small chickens are released as substitutes[12]. Another evil spirit called Axhashong who is the giver of sudden death. If a man died unexpectedly, blood issuing from his mouth and nostrils, no illness having preceded it, his death is ascribed to axhashong.[13]

The Western Rengmas believe that a rich man has a sort of familiar being (khapui, aketsong) which brings him luck. It is spoken of as his dog, and is believed to be like a black dog with a white chest. It lives in its owner's house, and usually lies either near the bed in the inner room or near the basket in which rice husks are put in the outer room. Sometimes, it will sleep in a granary, and the hollows in the pile of rice used by these spirits as resting-places are pointed out. It is only visible in dreams, but strangers have to be careful not to anger it. For this reason, a guest in a rich man's house never sits either near the bed or near the husk basket, so that he may not block the doorway in case the 'dog' wants to go out. If a man angers the familiar being unknowingly, he will be struck dumb and his eyes will stare. This is said to have happened to Hepegha and Rillo at the funeral of Kesatha, a rich man of Tseminyu, although they sat by the hearth after its owner's death till it was demolished when it disappeared.

The equivalent among the Eastern Rengmas is a spirit they call Ashupu (the catcher). It is believed that in the olden days rich man used to woo these spirits, but the last known case occurred before Meluri was founded. The peculiarity of the 'Catches' was that it held immovable any one who tried to steal from the house of the rich man it was protecting.[14]

Lycanthropists

Though very rare, Rengmas have been in their ancient days, confirmed lycanthropes. The theory and symptoms are clear and recognizable, and, differing from lycanthropes in many parts of the world. The Rengma undergoes no physical change whatsoever. The 'possession', if we may term it so, is not induced by any external aid, but ordinarily comes on at the bidding of spirits which may not be gain-said and under whose influence the man possessed losses entirely his own volition in the matter. The habit is very far from desired. No one wants to be possessed by the habit and it is, on the contrary, feared as a source of danger and a great weariness to the flesh.

The soul usually enters the tiger or leopard during sleep and returns to the human body with daylight. However, it may remain in the tiger for several days at a time, in which case the human body, though conscious, is lethargic. It (i.e., the human body) goes to the fields and follows the usual routine of life but is not able to communicate intelligent with other persons until the possession expires for the time being. The soul, however, is conscious, more or less, of its experiences in tiger form and can, to some extent, remember and relate them when it has returned to its human consciousness. During sleep, the soul is the tiger with its full faculties, but when the human body is wide awake, the soul is only semi-conscious. If at all, it is aware of its doings as a leopard unless under the influence of some violent emotion such as fear, experienced by the leopard, or tiger.

The possession is accompanied by very severe pains and swellings in the knees, elbows and smell of the back the human body, both during, and consequent to the possession. These pains are such as would result from far and continuous marching or from remaining for long periods in an unaccustomed position. During sleep at the time of possession the limbs move convulsively, as the legs of a dog move when it is dreaming. When the tiger is being hunted by man, the human body behaves like a lunatic, leaping and throwing itself about in its efforts to escape. Under these circumstances, the relatives of the were-tiger feed him with ginger as fast as possible in order to make him more active. So that the tiger body, on which his life depends may have the agility to escape its pursuers. When the tiger is wounded, corresponding wounds appear upon the human body of the were-tiger, and when the tiger is killed, the human body dies. It is, however, possible apparently for the soul to throw off the possessions permanently as old age approaches. Possession is not confined to man. Women also become were-leopards or were-tigers and one far more destructive as such than men are.[15]

Eschatology

All the Naga beliefs are concerning the existence of soul after death. Every tribe has a definite belief, and shares of meat, rice beer were always laid for the souls of the dead during festivals and other religious ceremony. The soul (Aghamuo /Kapu) of the dead man does not at first know that he is dead. Then he sees his own body lying on the outer room ready for burial, and understands why his relations and friends were weeping. He hangs about the house till the Ngada/Akhu ceremony which marks the close of the year[16]. Refreshed by the food and drink offered then, the soul goes to the land of the Hades[17] (Teronyu phong; Keshünu). The Kentennenyu clan, which is known to be of fairly recent sema origin, take a different route from the Asonyu clans and go to Sihama, an Angami village to the South-West, and there enters the earth-quite how is not known. The Journey is believed to take three days, and it is believed that souls need to send up a smoke signal from Sinhama to tell their friends of their arrival. All other clans go to Wokha Hill and enter the earth by the road of the Dead (Teronyu Tsong or Dicüü) used by the Lothas[18]. The Eastern Rengmas believe that a soul of the dead goes to the region from where they split. With them they take those of their worldly possessions (or the "souls" of them) that have been buried with them or placed on their graves, and all the mithun or other animals they have sacrificed or killed during life, accompany them[19]. After the death of a rich men, a dog and a chicken were sacrificed, it is believed that the spirit of the dog will park and defend the soul, whereas the chicken will crow and lead the dead soul to the land of death[20]. At the entrance to the cave by which they enter stands a woman called Azati[21]. By whichever route they go all clans meet below the earth[22]. On the way there a man meets all the enemies and animals he has killed at his funeral and he barks and frightens them away. His clans' men, too, help him, for men of all clans are waiting by the road, and as each soul passes it is asked to what clan it belongs, and is then escorted by its own relations. It is a thirsty road, but the funeral chicken scratches in the ground and the water flows forth. The Semas believes that when the dead man reaches the land of the dead, wherever that is he goes to his own village, of which there is presumably a ghostly reproduction, and lives just as he did in this life, after presuming the thief of the village with the chicken which he takes with him for the purpose. Before, however, he reaches that land he must pass by the house of the spirit Litsomo or Kolavo, which is alongside the road of the Dead. The spirit seizes and devours the souls of the unwary, and perhaps for this reason a man takes his spear and shield to the grave. A young boy is not buried without a sharpened bamboo. Jungle and creepers block the way, and a girl who dies a virgin will have no one to help her to track a path through[23]: When a lover on earth mopes and falls sick after the death of his beloved, it is believed that his soul is away helping her along the road of the dead and clearing her way for her. Tiny children are met by a good spirit called Samazi who carries the little children, and in the Tesophenyu group of villages each is given at death a rough bamboo fan (Awhentsa) to hold in front of its face so that it shall not see water and be frightened. This is put with other death offerings outside the front wall of the house. Those who were poor here are poor there, and those who gave feasts of Merit here give them again in the world below. Those who were unmarried here remain so there. Thieves and wicked men remember their sins and are unhappy, and the good live in joy. Including this world there are seven worlds in layers as it were, one below the other. A man, therefore, is born and dies seven times in all. At the last death those who could sing will become crickets on this earth, and those who could not will become butterflies[24]. For this reason, grown men and women do not kill butterflies and crikets, though nothing seems to be done to stop children doing so. Rich man becomes an ant whereas the poor turns to withered *calicarpa* leaves. Especially are people careful not to kill the large black swallow-tail with red and white marking, as these are believed to be the souls of rich men, the pattern on the wings representing that on the cloth given at the great feast of Merit.

The Eastern Rengma belief is very simple and vague, they are content to know that their dead go back to the ancestral home of the tribe, and there meet the fate of the other dead, though what that fate is they have forgotten. They say that the soul (sumetu) goes to the land of Western Rengmas in the form of a hawk (Alanyi)[25]. There it lives its life over again in the village of the dead, though whether that village is in this world or below is not known. After four or five lives the soul just ceases to be. Together with this belief is held an entirely inconsistent one in re-incarnation. For three or five months after a death no one of a dead man's family will kill a bird or a butterfly. In case it is the dead man, besides, the soul proper they believe in a "Birth spirit" which lives in a man and protects him throughout life and dies when he dies. The Western Rengmas hold that animals also have souls, but the Eastern Rengmas know of no such belief[26].

Ancestor Worship

The term ancestor worship describes, in a broad and loose sense, a variety of religious beliefs and practices concerned with the spirits of dead persons, regarded as relatives, some of who may be mythical. Although far from universal, ancestral worship exists or formerly existed in societies at every level of cultural development.

Ancestor worship is found in many societies throughout the world, especially where the local community is composed of kin-groups who believes themselves to be descended from a common ancestor. The ancestors are often thought of as guardians of the community and the health of herds' animals. They are believed to punish crimes, breaches of the moral code, and infringement of the custom by sending sickness, drought or crop diseases which can only be counteracted by appropriate sacrifice and ceremony of prayers[27]. The dead ancestors now passed into a deity, simply goes on protecting his own family and receiving suit and service from them as of old. The dead chief still watches his own tribe, still holds his authorities by helping friends and harming enemies and still rewards the right and sharply punishes the wrong. In this view of the case the departed ancestor is regarded as invariably kindly and well disposed towards his surviving relatives, and it may be said that this is the usual feeling of savage and barbaric man towards his kings-folk who had passed into the other world. W.R. Smith states, "Primitive sacrifice is an act of communion, the totem animal or beast sacred to the god being slain in order to renew or re-establish the bond of connection between the clan and its supernatural ally".

In the cultures that practice ancestor worship the living and the dead are much related as any other two classes of a given community, for death does not make a person cease to belong to his social unit (family/clan/village, tribe and nation). The respect of elders is so deep, which even the death cannot melt. In this regard, a close relation with the ancestors continues through worship. The dead may be regarded as friendly, as kindred beings with whom kindly relations are possible; they may be for a time displeased and angry with their people, but such displeasure may be dispelled when proper respect, reverence and worship are manifest. The dead, spirits of the deceased strangers, as levelent spirits of the deceased, may also be regarded unfriendly to the living persons of a given community, as malevolent spirits capable of rendering harm to individuals or to the entire community[28].

Attitude towards the spirits of the dead vary from love, respect, and trust mingled with special feelings of reverence, to outright fear; the attitude are sometimes ambivalent. Not all ancestors are equally worthy of worship, for some are regarded as being more powerful than others. Ordinary members or a group, when dead, are tended only by their immediate relatives or perhaps not at all or not for very long, while the spirits of great personages or warriors become the focus for more elaborate cultic expression by an entire community[29]. Seniority as well as prominence may have brought about the emergence of a dead person to the rank of a worshipped ancestor. Depending on the manner in which kin are organized into social groups, ancestral spirits that are worshipped may be limited or are limited to male lines among the Rengmas. The founder of a family, for example, may be worshipped by that family for an indeterminate number of generations.

Ancestral spirit may be called upon to assist the community of the living in many ways; to assure the continuation of the life to avert illness or plague; to assist in the obtaining of good crops; to assist in the war against the enemies[30]. In many cultures ancestors are viewed as living in the ground; to intercede with gods; since they are associated with gods and often are viewed as living in the sky or in the abode of deities[31]. On the contrary, it is admitted that fear of the dead was and is equally widespread, and is equally natural. It is universally admitted that the spirits of stranger and enemies are inimical, and the same feeling is extended to those who have perished by an untimely death, or in some unusual or tragic way.[32]

Priesthood

As ritual observances and sacrificial practices gradually became too complicated for the average man to master, a professional priesthood became necessary, when the people were uncertain about the proper ceremonies, they applied to the more experienced practitioners asking them to perform the ceremonies on their behalf. Kindred customs may be one reason for the old men officiating as priests among the Naga tribes.[33] Certain facts show how, especially on important occasions, the task of performing religious ceremonies seems to have been put into the hands of priests, or of those possessing most experience in the tribe; at the same time everyone was supposed to know how to sacrifice for ordinary private purpose, as regards the knowledge imparted to the candidates, mere theoretical learning is little thought of. According to our scanty reports, most importance is attached to practical knowledge which may be of use in the religious performances.

Though there was no monarchical system prevail among the Rengma, villager whose qualifications are membership of the right clan, performing in completion the full series of personal ginnas which determine social standing and skill in the rules of sacrifice, prayer, purification and close communication with the ancestors, is considered as the chief priest of the village. He is also regarded as the head of the village; where village matters other than religious are decided by him. He announces all the community ceremonies, like the clearing of the village, paths, agricultural ceremonies and others. Besides, all the individual performances will be announced by him. In most of the individual religious ceremonies, he will be called to perform, whom other religious officials of the host clan will assist. He is, from the point of view of religious ceremonies, the most important person in the village.[34] Nevertheless, his post is neither permanent nor hereditary. He being the eldest among the priests is appointed or chosen as the head of the village. All the men who have completed the full series of religious sacrifices and upped the mithun sacrifice (Asie Keyathi) are called the priest or religious officials (Asi Kesa). They are highly recognized by the people and receive the highest social status in the community. They also act as secular officials in the village.

Among some people every individual still performs his religious rites for himself without the assistance of professional priest within the separate families, in which, as has been pointed out, ancestral God is practically worshipped, one member is generally invested with the duty of sacrificing for the whole family. As a rule, the priestly functions are put in the hands of the pater familias, and the reasons seem to be that he is the eldest and most experienced male member of the family, who is generally believed to stand in closer communication with the ancestors than the other members. Sometimes the eldest female member of the family may also officiate as priest.[35] For example, on the tenth day of a child's birth, the mother will act as her own priest and perform the purification ceremony. Likewise, in most of the minor religious rites, an individual becomes his or her own priest.

One circumstance, which has powerfully tended to distinguish the priesthood from the community at large, has been the fact that the priests are, as a rule, recruited from the most intelligent elements of their people. The scanty learning of savage races is almost exclusively confined to the priest, who is generally the only preserver of tribal traditions; they alone possess the knowledge of certain useful arts, and the whole character of their functions tends to develop their intellectual powers and to give them superiority over their fellow-tribesman. Consequently the task of performing the services which every community as a whole owed to its gods would have developed upon, or been deliberately deputed to, a special body of men[36].

Purification

Among the more prominent factors both in the regulation of primitive life and in the determination of the character of religious ritual are the conceptions of the state of purity and the attendant ceremonies requisite for the preservation of that state, and for its recovery should it be impaired. It must be noted, however, that purity as conceived by the primitive mind has a wider significance than is usually attached to the modern use of the term among civilized people, in which emphasis is laid on the positive side of its meaning, purity being almost regarded as the equivalent of continence or chastity. The difference is sometimes expressed by applying to the primitive idea the epithet "Ceremonial" and further by printing out the non-ethical character of ceremonial purity or ceremonial uncleanness. But apart from the question whether it is correct to deny the term 'ethical' to any body of rules governing conduct, it would be more correct to describe ceremonial purity as pre-ethical in that, as will appear, in certain respects it provided the basis for higher moral codes.

Owing to the emphasis on the negative and inhibitory aspect, which is generally characteristic in primitive action, which purification ceremonies have as their object protection from harmful influence rather than attainment of righteous even of ceremonial kin? The state of purity would be defined by the primitive savages as one which resulted from such a course of action that defilement whether by intentional or by inadvertent act, had been avoided[37].

Ceremonial purity is closely bound up with the class of ideas and rules of conduct described by the general term 'taboo'. Infringement of taboo, whether voluntary or involuntary, renders the individual subject of spiritual influences. As such he not only is a danger to himself, but may transmit the dangers to others, and may affect the whole community. Hence, certain restrictions are imposed upon him. He is isolated; his actions are regulated that they may not affect the well-being of the community.

Ceremonial defilement is closely connected with the occasions of crises in human life, both social and natural, such as birth, initiation, puberty, marriage, and death. Death to the primitive mind is the greatest pollution of all, so much so that it commonly puts an end for a time to all activity over a social circle of varying extent. Unnatural dead bodies (fall of the tree, killed by tiger, etc.) will not be brought inside the village; and that body is buried separate from the village cemetery. Except some relatives of the deceased, none will neither help nor watch the burial function. It becomes taboo to call the name of the deceased thereafter. The implements used for burial of the dead body will be thrown away or kept on the grave.

The wide-spread custom of placing implements, weapons, etc in the grave for the use of the spirit is also no doubt to some extent an outcome of an idea that they are unlucky, while the custom almost equally wide-spread, of avoiding the use of the name of the deceased is based on a disinclination to afford an opportunity for an adverse influence to make itself felt by the use of a word which is associated with the unclean. Such possessions as are not devoted to the spirit of the dead are frequently destroyed.

For many purification ceremonies, an individual will be his or her own priest, and for others, calls in an old man. Among the Eastern Rengmas, after each series of feast of merit ceremonies; the husband and wife will go to the river, where they bathe for purification of the body. In most of the individual and common ceremonies, they observe purification rites for house of the whole community. Some of the most important ceremonies are mentioned here. Every year the Rengmas observe Agidsen giton ceremony where the weapons and implements will be cleaned and rites are performed by the men folk. The whole village will stay home without any work and have an individual family feast. One very important event is sleeping in the jungle (Aghaajaa Kejen) by the male members (including the young boys). Except sickness, all male members must join hand. After every seven years this is practiced. Each clan will make its own fountain, from where the all members will sanctify the body by washing face, hands, legs, and the corners of their cloths, including their implements. For the young boys, their respective fathers help them. For fear of ceremonial defilement, the Rengmas strictly maintain the religious code.

Notes and References

1. Milada Ganguli, *A Pilgrimage to the Nagas*, 1984, p. 89.
2. Like other tribes, this ceremony was conducted at the end of the year, mostly when the harvest was finished.
3. Gazetteer of India, Nagaland, Tuensang District, 1981, p. 40.
4. More or less the gods of Hindu pantheon.
5. Elwin Verrier, *The Nagas with 19th Century*, 1969.
6. The Semas and the Angamis have the same version.
7. The writer had faced this several times. When this spirit attacks, sense will remain normal, but feels sleepy, people talking can be heard, but calling out for help is not possible. Except for toes, the whole body becomes immobile.
8. J.P. Mills, *The Rengma Nagas*, p. 166. Azang = Ayen, Satsatetsu = Sakeditson.
9. Certain Angami and Lotha clans or kindred claim decent from such person. A Phom clan is likewise descended from a woman of the same sort who was found in a cave. In 1914, a Konyak village was reported to have actually caught a junglé spirit in a snare and thrown its body away.
10. Usually at night the same are heard like the chicken calling her hen or ringing the bell.
11. In 1956, my father saw the snake, about 2-ft long having multicolour. His parents did not allow him to profess Christianity, but he forcefully went to other village attending services and while coming, on the way he met the snake, he nearly died of suffering
12. J.P. Mills, *The Rengma Nagas*, p. 167.
13. *The Angami Nagas*, p. 182.
14. *The Rengma Nagas*, p. 168.
15. *The Sema Nagas*, p. 201-05.
16. See page of Ngada 110.

17. Lotha, Sema and Ao beliefs the same.
18. *The Rengma Nagas*, p. 165. The eastern Semas also used this road.
19. The Angamis, Maos, Chakesangs also did the same.
20. See page 51.
21. *The Rengma Nagas*, p. 170
22. The Change too believe future world is underground.
23. See the *Ao Nagas*, p. 228
24. See the *Sema Nagas*, p. 211, The *Ao Nagas*, p. 226.
25. The *Ao Nagas*, p. 226
26. The *Rengma Nagas*, p. 171.
27. Tseminyu sacrifice human being
28. Such ceremonial worship was manifest in the Roman cult of the masses.
29. An apparent example is Asclepius, worshipped in many parts of Greece as a god but also spoken as a hero.
30. Spearing enemy's effigy day, offer meat and drinks to the ancestors.
31. *The New Encyclopaedia Britannica* Vol. 1 Micropaedia, p. 1768.
32. On this principle Frazer (GB2; 331) explains the inconvenient restrictions imposed on the victors in their hour of triumph after a successful battle in obedience to which the warrior is isolated for a period from his family, confined to a special hut, and compelled to undergo bodily and spiritually purification.
33. Kiangans in Luzon, tribes in India. Africa and Australia; practiced the same culture.
34. For the benefits of the agricultural products, the Kandinu villagers kept two chief priests who will assist one another. Among the Tseminyu group, at the first harvest a woman did the ceremony.
35. Among some lower Dravidian tribes the family worship is conducted either by the head of the household or by the son-in-law or brother-in-law.
36. James Hastings, *Encyclopaedia of Religion and Ethics*. Vol. 1. p. 286.
37. James Hastings, *Encyclopaedia of religion and Ethics*. p. 455.

Chapter 3

Animal Hunting

Like other Naga tribes, the Rengmas too love hunting for the meat it brings, the sports it gives them and social status it lifts to a higher rank. Certain number of genna regularly observed in connection with hunting, some of which are as same as those observed in the case of head-hunting or war. If luck in hunting departs from a village the Western Rengmas observe one day's 'genna' called Phukens (A) or Kemini (B). Men must keep entirely apart from women for twenty-four hours. The Eastern Rengmas have no 'genna' for hunting[1]. Guns being scarce in the Rengma Country[2], spear and dao are carried on regularly, for the hunting was done mostly by a group with hunting dogs. As usual the eldest men among the party consult the omen not just testing for luck alone but also to avoid accident. Sometimes they postpone the programme seeing the bad omen. The nature of omen is determined by slicing the branch of 'Akhashü' lot tester, and when the slices fell on the ground facing the cut mark at the sky, it is considered to be good and vice-versa[3]. There are a certain number of genna regularly observed in connection with hunting, some of which approximate very closely to those observed in the case of war or head-taking.

Who ever kills tiger, elephant, bear, wild boar and other big animals must remain chaste for fifteen days and will not eat rice on those days[4], also in case of hunting animals like deer and stag and the killer will abstain from rice for ten days. Some villages remain chaste for ten days and no genna for small animals. He must sleep at Morung (azüüghüü),[5] on a bed of split bamboo to prevent sound sleep, during which the soul of the slain beast might attack and devour his own. The Eastern Rengmas may not eat rice for five days. He will have to make a separate well and drink from the new well till the genna is over; at the same time he will sleep in the morung. Whoever touches him will have to sleep one night in the morung. For one month the killer of the tiger will not eat any kind of meat. Like the Angamis it is generally held to be genna for a man to eat game killed by whatever means by him until he has killed 100 or 150 heads, excluding little birds and quite small mammals[6].

When the genna is over a gourd filled with rice beer and cooked meat wrapped in banana leave is carried to the jungle for an offering ceremony to God. Nobody will be allowed to see him; he cleans the spot after which the wrapped meat is untied and put some pieces of meat on the new leaves laid as offering to God. As usual practice of the Rengmas, he will hold the beer cup and blow off the upper layer on the ground; that is the share of God[7].

He will offer words of prayer, thanking God for protecting him from the mouth of enemies and seeking blessing for the life to live[8]. He eats meat and drinks the rice beer and returns home without doing any other work. On reaching home he makes a new hearth which is covered with bamboo mat avoiding family members to see him cooking and eating. He will cook rice, and bamboo-shoot curry on the new hearth and will eat alone in the evening like the head-hunting genna he will not eat creeper leaves for seven years and for the rest of life he will not eat soyabean, oilseeds and mushrooms[9].

The two animals, Tiger, and leopard are hardly distinguished, and both are mystic beasts, sharing a common ancestry with man. Special ceremonies therefore follow the killing of one, and a man never admits having done so himself, though he will wear the ornaments[10] to which the feat entitles him, which among the Eastern Rengmas are the same as those won by killing a man. Who kills a tiger at a village hunt is never mentioned as having done so, and will not himself boast of his deed. He will merely say, "The village kills a tiger". When a man, in these days of guns, shoots one he says when he comes home, "I have sounded an animal"[11]. Like the Sema the dead body of leopard and tiger is treated much as that of an enemy, the head being taken back to the village and hung up outside the village gates.

As one would expect in the section of the tribe that uses dogs, an annual ceremony is performed to increase their chances of success. This takes place in January, on the day after the great zü-kulu ceremony[12]. On that day all owners of hunting-dogs assemble with their dogs at some spot well away from a path and unlikely to be visited by a woman, for her presence would bring ill luck to an essentially male sport. Some water is brought, and the face and paws of each dog are formally washed, and their bodies are brushed ten times with a sevenfold brush used for illness while the following words are uttered: "Your nose must be keen; if animals came from Japfü Hill you must track them; if animals come from Wokha Hill you must track them; if animals come from the plains you must track them; if animals come from the East you must track them".

Then a small chicken is killed and a fire is lighted. The chicken must have been seized in the morning without permission from anyone, as if it were a wild bird, though the owner is told in the evening and paid. This is signed and offered by the oldest man present to the spirit of game, ten scraps being placed on santsu leaves to his right hand and nine to his left. Next, the omen for the year is taken as follows. The oldest man stands up facing the East and away from the village and all spears are put into his arms. He suddenly spills them on the ground to his front, and the man whose spears shoot farthest forward will get most game. Firstly, all pass through the fire, first dogs and then bitches, and then men in order of age. All then go hunting in the jungle[13]. All the skulls of larger animals killed by him are religiously kept, even that of an elephant, while the heads and legs of small birds may often be seen nailed to his house.

Head-Hunting

Head-hunting as an accompaniment of the blood feud and of war has been mentioned, but so much significance has been attached to the practice that it possibly deserves some special notice. Head hunting in one form or another is wide-spread practice whatever the various incidents of head-hunting in various quarters of the globe.[14] The ultimate reason of its existence in any particular spot must probably be sought in some deep-rooted and innate characteristic of human nature[15]. "Truly the ...merry head-hunter... reduced art and philosophy is a single code. To take your adversary's head, to basket it at the portal of your castle, to see it lying there, a dead thing, with its cunning and stratagems and power gone – Is there a better way to foil his plots, to refute his arguments, to establish your superiority over his skill and wisdom?" Among the Naga tribes at any rate, head-hunting, though associated with a vague idea of the benefits accruing from human sacrifice, must also be connected in no small degree with ordinary, every day human vanity. What man, or at the least what Naga, who has killed his enemy does not want to boast about it? And unless he can show the body, where is the proof? Most savages are somewhat economical of truth? At any rate the Naga is when it comes to his exploits in war and the chase. If the slayer can produce the body of the slain his statement is likely to be accepted as true and since retrieving the body would be a laborious, not to say often dangerous proceeding, the head is naturally part of it to bring back as testimony, as it gives a definite assurance that the foe has been killed, not scotched[16], Moreover, it can be retrieved, the Rengmas does prefer the whole body, and if the whole body is not available he will take the arms, and legs, and feet of the corpse as well as its head. And in this connection it must also bot be forgotten that the Nagas does not fight in the open country and under the eyes of his fellows, but in heavy jungle and in raiding parties of small numbers from one upwards, where none can observe his deeds of daring. Nor does the Naga make so very radical a distinction between human heads and heads of game. Man is the biggest game and the most dangerous game, and his pursuit is therefore, attended with precautions which may be unnecessary in the case of the smaller game, but he is still game. Like the animal game, lot is consulted before going to raid the enemy[17]. The warriors have not only acquires land but also defend and retaliated the aggression of their neighbours. The Rengma, on the other hand, says bluntly and openly that enemy's heads cause the crops to flourish, and men and animal to increase. They therefore, feel enemies' heads to be a real need, and believed that they suffer loss of the fertility of soil if they lack them. They indulge in human sacrifice at times when they have been unable to obtain heads in war[18]. The wretched slave is tied up and is killed (Akuk village sacrificed slave the last among the Lothas)[19], and head hands and feets are hung from the head-tree as if they are those of an enemy killed in war. This custom brings us nearer to another idea which underlies head-taking, and that is the idea of sacrifice, the notion of community or of the crops[20]; in certain cases they are doing the most effectual thing towards averting the displeasure of some particular evil spirits.[21] Head-hunting might be occasioned by varied number of circumstances: a private feud, a land dispute or mere lust of blood anything[22].

The proper proceedings, preparatory to war, are opened by sending of messenger to the village with which the challenging village desired a trail of strength. This messenger would probably be as well versed in the dialect of the other village and known to them through trading operations if possible. He would challenge the village to do battle and would name the day, saying, "The man of my village will come on such and such a day. Our spears and daos are very long and sharp, our shields are very strong, come out and try if you can eat them". Some time the messenger would send the message through third village in order to avert the risk of his head being taken by his enemies. When the message reaches the challenged village, the informed hostility commences, then the eldest man in the village consults the usual omens by slicing a piece of the *Adhatoda zeylanica* Plant (Akhashü) on the ground. If the slicing cheese fall facing sliced marked upward, then the omen is good, after which the acceptance reply is sent. The warriors strictly maintain the norms of their religion, lest they die at enemy's hand. A man intending to go on a raid had to remain chaste, lest he should weaken himself, and might not catch up pigs and fowls, lest he become confused and rush wildly about like they do. While the husbands are away, their wives could not spin, or their man would trip over creepers, and had to remain chaste, or they would be killed or wounded. This was naturally to be avoided if possible though unlike some tribes, the Rengma do not consider death in war to be disgraceful[23].

The challenging village would come, but first lighted a fire and sat down to wait. When the enemy arrived, they would light fire a short distance away. Both sides being in full dress and armed with shield would clear the battlefield of jungle. When this was done, the fight began with each side throwing eggs at the other for the thrower of an egg rid himself of ill-luck and danger of being wounded. There was far more shouting and abusing each other than real fighting, but edged weapons were used and blood was let. There was no fighting to the last man, however, eventually, one side or other, finding itself lacking in number or in courage, would take bodily to flight, often throwing away their weapons in the panic. Honour was satisfied with very few casualties, unless one was seized with a panic early in the proceedings, so that the other side was able to pursue in large numbers.

Most fighting, however, was not in this manner. Usually a party of braves would go out either to snatch a head or two from a sleeping village or more commonly, to try to rush the sentries guarding a party working in the fields and fall upon the screaming women as they scattered. It stimulated the crop to grow better, especially when the head was that of a woman with long hair[24]. It is well recognized fact that the village which gets the first blow in this manner scores heavily, whereas after both sides are on the lookout for raids, it is difficult to get more than two or three at a time. After this, the war would become a mere series of head taking with no formality, carried on by both sides according to impulse and opportunity. The heads were taken to the village, the party burst into songs and shouts as they approached the village and everyone swarmed out to meet and congratulate them. The tired and thirsty warriors, who had probably run hard, even if they had not fought hard, were refreshed with food and drink outside the village fence, and went straight to the head-tree, usually somewhere near the edge of the village, where they chanted the wordless chant. Time being needed to prepare for the ceremony of hanging up the heads it did not take place till the next day. Meanwhile the raiders, being in a sense unclean, could not go to their house, and the whole party had to sleep in the morung "azüüghüü", the heads being put on a ledge of the Totem post "aghon". Neither the hands and weapons of the warriors could be washed[25], and, to avoid touching food with blood stained hands they have to convey food to their mouths with a special *Rhusemialata* spoon and stiff *Thaumaloeccus* leaf cup. The ceremony was observed the next day, a pig and a dog were sacrificed, and the meat shared by all who had taken part in the raid. After then, the heads were taken to the head-tree with much chanting and war cry and hung from it in the presence of the whole village, which was genna day for the whole village. To hang it up a stick was driven through it from side to side behind the temples. A cane string was attached to each of the stick and the two ends were tied to a long string hanging from a bamboo set to lean against one of the branches of the head-tree[26]. When the head had been hung up, an old warrior of note addressed to it the following prayer that other heads might soon hang beside it[27]. "May those who do not obey their parents come and seek for you here. May rich men of your village, may wicked men, may proud men come and seek you."[28] The whole village remained genna for five days, which were spent feasting and rejoicing and the raiders spend fifteen nights at morung and used separate hearths. The genna for the killers of the enemies are as same as the killer of big animals.[29] For fifteen days the raiders drank only rice beer and ate sacrificed meat, cooked without chilly. On the sixteenth day, all the warriors filled their gourd cups, wraped the cooked meat in *Thaumaloeccus* leaf and carried it to the jungle for religious rites. Each warrior would go to a very secret place where meat and rice beer was offered to God along with prayer. The remaining meat and beer was eaten and drunk by him and he returned home. In the evening he would cook in a separate hearth and eat alone. The new hearth was fenced with bamboo mats. If he did not do this, it is believed they would never get heads again. He will not eat creepers for seven years, and for the rest of his life he will abstain from eating oil seeds, soybeans and mushroom as it is believed that eating such crops will lead them to mental disorder or madness.

Head hunting prevailing in the past had religious sanction and economic usefulness, and it had special value. For instance, when the warriors brought the enemy's head, the whole village rejoiced and paid great honour to them. The young warriors who scored a number of heads over their rivals were admired the most by the girls and had a better chance of getting the fairest wife.[30] They were entitled to wear a special type of shawl which ordinary men were not allowed to wear. However, head hunting like those of the other Naga tribes became extinct with the coming of British Administration and the Gospel of Christ.

Notes and References

1. J.P. Mills. *The Rengma Nagas*, p. 95.
2. From Lt. A.E. Woods I.S.C Assistant Commissioner, Naga Hills, No. 24; Dated 8/5/1892.
3. The Angamis, Lothas and Semas practice the same culture.
4. The Semas do not eat one day, but remain chaste for six days.
5. Practiced by Phenshünyu villagers.
6. Hutton, *The Angami Nagas*, p. 84.
7. Lotha practiced the same. See the *Lotha Nagas*, p. 109.
8. The prayers are different from person to person.
9. It is believed that these vegetables have so many germs which is eaten by the common people as their main food items.

10. A man who first spears at the tiger, killing it, wears his three small circles of cowries (tiger's eye) on the black cloth at the top of his apron.
11. The *Ao Nagas*, p. 297.
12. An important ceremony of the Southern Group and of the Eastern Group, corresponding exactly to the Angami Sekhrienyi. The *Angami Nagas*, p. 203.
13. *The Rengmas Nagas*, p. 101.
14. Some recent writers on the tribes of North Borneo have sought for an explanation of the practice in a desire for the hair for the ornamentation of the shield and the Sword-hit, or in the custom of killing slaves to accompany dead chief beyond the grave.
15. It is worth quoting from Mr. O. Henry.
16. *The Angami Nagas*, p. 157.
17. See page 37.
18. Northern Rengma do not practice human sacrifice.
19. *The Lotha Nagas*, p. 109.
20. The Angami feels the same; see *The Angami Nagas*, p. 159.
21. Mr. A.W. Davis, writing in 1898 as Deputy Commissioner of the Naga Hills.
22. T.C. Hodso wrote; it must also be borne in mind that the successful issue of a raid at the beginning of the cultivating season brings prosperity to the crops.
23. *The Angami Nagas*, p. 151.
24. Dr. Verrier Elwin, *The Nagas in the 19th Century*.
25. The Ilongots of the Philippines may not wash the blood off arms, body and legs after a head-hunting raid. See Savage Landor, *Gems of The East*, Vol., p. 330
26. The Angami hung up at the hunters' house. See *The Angami Nagas*, p. 162. The Aos and the Konyaks hung either at morung or hunter's house, or sometimes the Konyaks hung it at the chief's house.
27. For precise parallels, in N. America and W. Africa, see "*The Golden Bough*" Vol. III. pp. 236 and 244.

28. In Formosa too, an enemy's head is asked to bring others of its village to be killed. (McKay, From Far Formosa, p. 273.).

29. See p. 41.

30. R.R. Shimray, *Origin and Culture of Nagas,* 1985.

Chapter 4

Birth and Death Ceremonies

It is believed that there is a great foot path junction where the photographs of all the dead persons are placed. Before a baby is conceived in the mother's womb, spirit of the would-be person has to go there and choose one of the photographs. Thenceforward, a child is conceived in the womb of the mother. If a would-be person chooses the photograph of a rich and famous person, all the spirits of the dead will clap their hands and rejoice, whereas if a would-be person chooses the photograph of a poor person, all the spirits of the dead will cry. A person will exactly leave and face the same life of the dead. Rites surrounding the birth of a child are often a complex of distinct rituals that prescribe different behaviour on the mother, father, and relatives, non-familial members of the society, and with respect to the newborn. Observances may begin when pregnancy is first noted and may continue until the time of delivery, when the full rite of passage is observed, and for a variable period of time afterwards. In addition to the articles of food which women are forbidden to eat at all times, there are certain other things that are prohibited during pregnancy. Both the husband and wife will neither touch nor eat meat of animals like bear, porcupine, fox and the like. And if the husband eats any of those things he must sleep apart for the following night.[1] To prevent harm to their children and other people during the ritual period, the parents observe foot taboo; eat in seclusion: avoid contact with other people and refrain from various other acts of ordinary behaviour that include cooking, touching tools and eating chilly and ordinary meat. Rites directed towards the new born similarly symbolize or ensure health and well-being and, after some days, week or months have passed, often include sacrifice or other ritual acts that introduce the child to supernatural beings. Both child and mother are often regarded as being defenseless at this time and many ritual acts have the purpose of protecting them from harmful supernatural beings and forces.[2]

In order to avert the guest from entering the house, certain leaves such as *Inula cuppa* (Shongphighi), *Occinum Bacilicum* (Chülakhwen) and *Elcholtzia strobilifera* (Ashenshü) are put in crevices at the side walls of the door. The same leaves are burned with the husk of the paddy in front of the house, believing that the smell of the leaves burned will cast away the evil spirit. Birth takes place in the back of the inner room of the house. The woman crouches for the delivery and is attended by some experienced woman usually her mother or mother-in-law, as mid-wife. As soon as the child touches the floor, the mother dabs a little spittle on its forehead and says, "It is mine". The baby is washed with warm water on the day of its birth by the mid-wife. When all is over, among the Eastern Rengma father comes and blesses his child by putting a little boiled rice in its mouth[3] saying "Live happily; be strong; be rich; be healthy."[4] The members of the household and the midwife may not work in their own fields or go to their granary. The father places three stones in position and makes a new hearth a little away from the general hearth[5]. He lights a fire with a fire-thong and cooks in a new rice pot and a fowl—a cock for a boy and a hen for girl—which he must kill with his own hand. The mother eats this meal only, and she uses this hearth for three days. It is taboo to eat the leftover of the curry[6] for ten days. The whole family remains genna for three days; for ten days, nothing in the house can be touched by anyone who is not an inmate, and the parents speak to no strangers.[7]

The child is named after three days. Before it the father fetches water and bathes the child. Then ornaments are kept near the baby and the baby is named from a selection of names current in clan. It must not include that of anyone who has died an unnatural death or, in the northern group, has had his head taken in war, is mad etc. The father takes omen with chips of wormwood (Akhashü) to see which are lucky. If no name in the father's clan seems to be of good omen, further selection is made from the mother's clan. Whichever clan has to provide names, the selection is made by old men of the father's clan, who meet at the parents' house. The names are eventually given to the child, but of these one is ordinarily never used.[8] This name is not secret in the strict sense, and it is not taboo to reveal it. Yet a man ordinarily does not know the second names of the brothers and sisters, or even of his own wife.

The Eastern Rengmas are supposed to name a boy after the sixth day of birth and a girl on the fifth. But this rule is not adhered to, and the whole business is most casual. No omens are taken, and anyone in the village seems to be at liberty to suggest a name, the parents finally deciding on the one they fancy most.

When the days of genna are completed, on the eleventh morning, she will cook rice and kill a cock for the male child and a hen for the female child, which is cooked with ginger and salt. She requires a young girl (Baby-sitter) from the relative who carries the basket filled with food items and goes with the former. The mother carrying the newborn child in the front will go with the baby-sitter to the outskirts of the village pretending that she is going to field. On her way she will throw the feathers by the side of the path.

And when she reaches a proper place, she says "this is my field" and eats the food items they were carrying and then returns to the house.[9] From then on, the child can be carried at the backside. She informs all her relatives that she will visit them with the child on the twelfth day. Accordingly, she visits them with the child; everyone welcomes them and presents a gift to the child. But when any house is found empty or without any member it is considered as bad omen for the child. Except females, the lobe of the ear pierced in the male child is not common among the Rengmas. The lobe of the ear pierce genna is very simple. The hair cannot be cut until the ears have been pierced. A child's ears are pierced any time up to two or three months after birth.

The Eastern Rengmas are bound to postpone this till after the harvest. Then the eldest man of the child's clan pierces the ears. All the Rengmas agree that the piercing of the lobes of the ears is of the utmost importance, as a person with unpierced ears would not be recognised and welcomed by the relatives in the land of Hades. The time of cutting of the hair is more important then the piercing of the ears; a cock for the boy child and a hen for the girl child is killed to celebrate the ceremony. Father fetches the water and washes the child's head. The mother threads a bead on a single hair, which she cuts with a bamboo knife (Aghana) so that the beads fall to the ground. The bead is never picked up, and the bamboo knife, with the hair tied to it, is hidden in the house by the mother. Then the father or any other man from the same clan cuts the hair, shaving the head entirely or leaving a top-knot, according to the sex of the child. Eastern Rengma kills a pig for hair cutting ceremony. Every house-hold is given rice and meat wrapped in a leave. Those who eat it will have to eat just before they sleep, and after eating it, nothing they will be put inside their mouth. The moment comes at last when the most emperious taboos relating to the child are introduced into the community. He cannot as a rule, become a full-fledged member of the community until he has, years later, passed through the fishing ceremony, but he may be recognised as a portion, however, imperfect, of the family or clan emerging from the seclusion which follows his birth. The village men will organise fishing day ceremony for the young boys of seven to eight years of age. The village elders and young men take the boys to the river and catch the fish, but it is taboo for the boys to see their elders fishing. Therefore, they keep seclusion at the bank of the river. The boys are allowed to see only after the fishes are gathered in one place. They cook the fish and have a great feast with the rice beer after the elders have blessed feast. The remaining fish is distributed among them. Only after this ceremony the boys are given due recognition in the community membership, and are entitled to go for hunting, fishing etc. This day is called "Little genna".[10]

Death Ceremonies

Man is the only creature of God known to bury his dead. The fact is of fundamental significance. For the practice was not originally motivated by hygienic consideration but by ideas entertained by primitive peoples concerning human nature and destiny. This conclusion is clearly evident from the fact that the disposal of the dead from the earliest time was of a ritual kind. The primitive peoples not only buried their dead but they provided them with food and other equipment, thereby implying a belief that the dead still needed such thing in the grave.

All the tribes in southern Nagaland bury their dead. The obsequies are elaborate, the rituals being connected with funerary feast, sacrifice of animals, ceremonial mourning, offering of food to the deceased. James Hasting writes, "the Nagas of Assam, the corpse is watched with great care, and when decomposition sets in, quantities of spirits are thrown over it, whatever the deceased was in the habit of eating and drinking in his lifetime (such as rice, vegetables and spirits) is placed once a month on the ground before the dead body. At the time of mourning a great feast, consisting of liquor, rice and flesh of cows and buffaloes is prepared, and the members of the clan in war dress partake of it [11].

Among the Rengmas, as soon as a man dies, the village burrier along with the clansman washes his body[12]. In the case of woman this duty is performed by her relatives. After washing, the dead man is laid out upon the bed and covered from the eyebrows to the feet with his own cloth. A little parcel of rice wrapped in leaf is put in the dead man's left hand for him to eat on his way to the land of dead. The burier washes the cloths in which the corpse will be laid out, really washing the old dirty ones, but only dipping the edges of the new ones in water to make them ceremonially pure. The senior surviving member of household hands the buriers a small basket of husked rice. From this he selects one unbroken grain for each member of the household, and tying them all up in a leaf, puts them in a pot of water on the fire for a minute and pretends to cook them. He then opens the leaf, and each member of the family in order of seniority takes a grain and presses it against his chin and says, "There must be no more deaths. I do not wish it for the death again. It is finished." and puts it again in the leaf, which is hidden in the jungle when the family wash at the village spring after the funeral. The rites are observed to protect the deceased from demonic attack. Sometimes the purpose of the rites has been to guard the living from the contagion of death or the malice of the dead; for it has often been believed that the souls continues to remain about the body until the burial.

Preparation are then at once made for the funeral feast and for the funeral which always takes place in the afternoon after a man's death. The funeral feast is proportionate to the wealth of the deceased. The funerary party content themselves with feast when all is over of animals slain (pigs, cows and even mithun).[13]

When the body is ready, it is placed in the coffin, at its right hand being placed a spear and a 'dao', three 'panjis' and a fire stick, with thong and tinder on the left. Nothing, except her clothes and beads is buried with a woman. The corpse is buried at an ancestral clan sepulchre situated at the ancient village site. Another common mortuary custom is the burial of a live chicken in a small hole apart from the grave, unlike the Angami who bury it with the corpse[14]. The dead man is not left dependent on what water the chicken may find. He has to be given the wherewithal to buy some if need be, and for this purpose a pinch of salt wrapped in a piece of banana leaf is put between the first and second fingers of each hand and a bead tied to the middle finger of the hand. When the deceased is a man who has taken heads, or killed a tiger, a dog is tied up near the body in the house. This will go barking in front of the dead man and frighten from his path/ the spirits of the enemies or the tigers he has killed. It is therefore killed by a blow on the head[15] at the moment the body is carried through the door feet first, amid the weeping of relatives and preceded by a formal friend calling on the dead man not to be afraid,[16] as he will clear all enemies from his path for him. Personal belongings as in Angami case are also displayed over the grave, with lots of foodstuffs and rice beer. Fire is lighted over the grave for a few nights following the burial. The most favourite relishment of the Rengma dead person is beer and a dish of chicken or indigenous fish cooked with vegetables. Mourning continues for three days as in the case of other tribes'[17]. During this period the relatives or clan members of the deceased, if living in the same village, will not go to the field and will eat rice, meat and beer. All who come to sympathise with the bereaved family or help in the burial are fed. It is rarely done that if the dead man is a warrior or a rich man who had performed some stages of religious sacrifices, a semi-circular stone platform (Atuchüü) is built on the tomb or on the path from the village to the fields, from where the spirits of the dead watch and bless the people who work in them. This is done any day after his death, arranged by the son if he has one, in commemoration of the dead. The stone platform is generally made for the people to rest on it. Those who can afford, erect a monolith at the side of the dolmen. Except his wife, even the eldest son of the man who died after completing the full series of the feast of merit will neither take nor touch his belongings. The house will not be repaired even if his wife survives.

The customs of the Eastern Rengmas differ widely from those of the rest of the Rengmas. They have no clan burial places,[18] Rough semi-circular stone monuments are invariably built at every funeral by the Eastern Rengmas. As soon as life is extinct, the workers who fetched the water from the village well with bamboo bucket wash the body. Young children are buried in the floor of the house under the bed or in any corner where the ground is soft enough to dig and the grave will not be trampled on,[19] but adults either under the eaves outside the house or in the street just in front. The digging is begun by the oldest man of the clan – the man to whom go the heads of all the game killed – and is carried on by male relatives. Pigs are slain in accordance with the wealth of the chief mourners. The main task of the day is the building of a rough semi-circular stone platform (Asüthi) on the path from the village to the fields, from where the spirit of the dead man will watch and bless the crops and those who work in them. For the spirit, there is built on the platform a tiny house on very high poles, with a small bin containing a little of every kind of edible grain in front of it. If the dead man has done the buffalo sacrifice in the series of feast of merit, an upright stone about one and a half feet is planted on his asüthi[20]. Over the little house on the stone platform is erected a wooden frame about eight feet high from which are hung gourds representing the heads of enemies the deceased has killed, the skull of animals he has got, and animals sacrificed by him during his lifetime, and bunches of tare, edible gourds etc. In front of the platform, reeds are stuck in the ground, representing the women with which he had love affairs[21]. A piece of bamboo is set upright, the bottom sharpened and thrust into the earth, the top split, splayed out, and made into the form of a basket by interweaving of horizontal strips. This is used as a stand for a gourd of liquor. A bag filled with the materials the deceased use during his lifetime is hung on the wooden frame. In the evening, all the workers individually or in groups, place a little water on the broken earthen pot and make hot in fire. Everyone tests it by dipping one's finger and says, "There is no more death in the village," and then throws the pot. On the next day, a small quantity of paddy is dried and pounded for cooking in order to give to the deceased. When the share of the dead is laid on the grave, cow or pig is slain for feast in resemblance to the deceased. All the workers will come to take their share which is taken home to cook at their respective houses. Non-workers are invited to partake together as it is genna to keep the leftover.

When the festival season approaches, the son(s) of the rich man organise a ritual feast for their deceased father. They dig bamboo rats (ahiefüü) and bring home alive. All the relatives who come to join their feast will have to bring cock, bird, or any type of meat, with which they cooked, for feast. The household materials used by the man are gathered at one place, and then the live bamboo rat is killed and its blood is sprinkled on the materials. The killer (eldest) cooks the bamboo rat and eats it. He will put six pieces of liver and rice on Chonghinga leaves and then offer prayer to God. After this, the liver is cut into smaller pieces and thrown away to the spirit. He then, eats up all the remaining. Any leftover is thrown away.

To the Rengma in his natural state, suicide seems to be absolutely unknown, a striking contrast with the closely allied Lotha[22]. It is therefore, impossible to say how the body of an animist Rengma would be disposed off in such circumstances. For death by accident, by murder,[23] or poison, killed by animals, by drowning, by falling from a tree or by being crushed by a falling tree, by childbirth or by any of the unmarried person is well expressed on his death. The death of bachelor or spinster is worst treated than any other unnatural death. The whole village will observe ten days genna for going to field lest less harvest[24]. The unnatural dead body is not allowed to be buried at the clan's cemetery, all those who died by accident or others, have to be buried at the outskirts of the village. Generally, there will be not many sympathisers from the community to the bereaved family; even relatives will ignore it. In such cases some of the poor men of the village are engaged to bury the body,[25] to whom they will pay in terms of paddy or even to the extent of giving a field. The buriers have to sleep in the morung for three nights and will have to eat and drink outside the village until the genna is over. A person dying in the house[26] is not carried out through the normal door of the house, but through a hole cut in the back of the house. No ceremony of any kind is performed. It becomes genna to go near the burial place for some few days[27]. All his belongings will be thrown away. But the house is not demolished, nor valuable property such as cattle and rice abandoned. For the Eastern, the whole village observes a day genna to go outside the village[28]. The relatives of a drowned man abstain from eating fish for one month. The dead person can never be spoken of by name. When it is required to refer to him or her, they use "devoured by tiger", "dead in child birth" or some other appropriate term.

Notes and References

1. The anthropologists Alfred L. Kroeber (1876–1960) reported that among most of the many tribes of the aboriginal California, rites at childbirth were much alike for both mother and father.
2. *The New Encyclopaedia Britannica*, Vol. 26, p. 849.
3. The Lothas put a little boiled rice into its mouth; See *The Lotha Nagas*, p. 145.
4. *The Rengma Nagas*, p. 145.
5. The Angamis practice the same. *The Angami Nagas*, p. 214.
6. It is believed that when the child is grown up, the child and the left-over eater will hate each other
7. A similar taboo exists among the Lothas and Garos. See *The Lotha Nagas*, p. 146 and Cf. Major A. Playfair, *The Garos*, p. 23.
8. cf. *Angami Nagas*, pp. 218 and 219.
9. The Semas practiced similar culture. See *The Sema Nagas*, p. 233.
10. Rengma proper doesn't practice this culture.
11. James Hastings, *Encyclopaedia of Religion and Ethic*, p. 450.
12. Tour Diary of Captain H.W.G. Cole, I.S.C., Deputy Commissioner of the Naga Hills for the month of Oct. 1897.
13. Among Tseminyu group, first all the assembled clansmen have a meal.
14. The Northern Rengmas kill and throw it away when the corpse leaves the house instead of being buried alive.

15. In ancient Mexico the domestic Techichi was similarly killed to accompany its master. (Spence, quoting Clavigero, *Magic and Mysteries of Mexico*, p. 109).
16. Similar with the Angamis, See A.W. Davis, in Census of India, 1891. Vol. I.
17. Gazetteer of India, Nagaland, Kohima District, p. 66.
18. R. Brown, Narrative Report of the progress of the survey party, Naga Hills Season 1874.
19. J.H. Hutton Tour Diary of the Deputy Commissioner, Naga Hills for the year 1926. POL-B, No. 707-737.
20. *The Rengma Nagas*, p. 220.
21. See *The Sema Naga* p. 246, Note.
22. *The Lotha Nagas*, pp. 20, 82.
23. Death in war is not a genna.
24. The highest genna ever observed for death by the whole community.
25. Tour Diary of Captain H.W.G. Cole, I.S.C., Deputy Commissioner of the Naga Hills for the month of Oct. 1897
26. Like by birth or poisoned.
27. A.W. Davis, In Census of India 1891, Vol. I.
28. A tiger killed Tsuthoba of Meluri Village, in 1954. His whole village remained at home one day.

Chapter 5

Marriage and Divorce

It is assumed by anthropologists that marriage is one of the earliest social institutions invented by man, and as already noted, rites of marriage are observed in every historical known society. Their rites vary from extremes of elaboration to utmost simplicity, and these may be secular events or religious ceremonies. Sub–classes of rites of marriage, named and unnamed exist in many societies, beginning with societies of betrothal that requires complex formalities of transferred exchange of goods, which are often regarded as compensation to the bride's kin group for their lost family member. Ceremonies of dramatics sham 'capture' of the bride by the groom and his relatives and his friends have been common in both proletariat and literate societies. Marriage in these societies is seen by social analysts as a cooperative liaison between two different groups of kin, between which some feelings of hostility exist. Ceremonies of token capture are conducted even when betrothal and all other arrangements for marriage have long been completed to the express satisfaction of both sides, and the sham capture were interpreted as socially sanctioned channel or the expression, and relief of feeling or hostility between the two kin-groups[1].

For the continuity of human society, man and woman must come together under recognised rules of the society concerned, and have children of their own legitimate offspring of the partners. It is the first and permanent social institution. A marriage is regarded merely as a civil contract, and no religious ceremonies are performed[2]. To them the maintenance of family continuity is one's greatest responsibility to one's ancestors for failure to produce offsprings is considered to be unfortunate, as it means not only the end of the family line but also the death of all the ancestors as well. It is therefore, that he who does not marry was much talked about in the village. No man can set up house on his own without a wife, and every man, however poor, secures one. Cross-cousin marriage, viz., children of a brother and sister marrying, and parallel cousin marriage, viz., children of two sisters of two brother marrying are strictly avoided[3]. One marrying one woman at a time is the leading form of marriage. No Naga marries more than one wife, and if she dies, he is at a liberty to marry again[4]. On the rare occasions, a rich man takes a second wife. She is considered to be of definitely inferior status, and he almost always builds a separate house for her. Usually the first is recognised as the primary wife, she does not allow the second to live under one roof. As a result the latter becomes the day wife of the man. To enjoy the favours of the second wife, he has to meet her secretly in the jungle while her co-worker is busy with other works during the day. The second marriage is usually a non ceremonial one. A childless widow re-marriage in the Rengma is not discouraged[5]. In the event of her husband's death, the widow marries with the husband's brother or any other man that she likes to marry. But once celebrated with ceremony and formality is conferred, the primary husband's family becomes the permanent guardian of a widow. In this regard, marrying with other man, bride's price will go to the former husband's family whereas her right to use her dead husband's property will be cut off.

Marriage, as said above, is a very important social institution. That is why no society allows a couple to quietly pair off and start living as husband and wife. For marriage aims not only towards the fulfillment of sex-urge and social task of procreation but side by side it appears as a means for the solution of the problems created by the economic hardship of the primitive way of life. The life in the primitive society was and is so hard that it is not possible to cope with it without the active participation of womenfolk. A healthy, hard-working and socially acceptable wife with moral conduct is the most desirable in selecting the bride. Domestication and agriculture being the main economy of the primitive society, the parents take a great consideration of economy in match making. Again in choosing a family for one's daughter the first consideration is the economic condition of the would-be son-in-law. Agriculture being the main occupation of the primitive society, old men and women, and the young boys and girls form various teams, work together in the fields. As the sun rises showering beams of light through the crevices of the bamboo walls of their houses, all the young and old prepare for the day's work in the field work, the people start going in groups to the paddy fields, all in batches of ten and twenties. Young girls will carry their boyfriends' food, implements etc. they will chat, tease their beloved ones and exchange glances with their fiancées and their girlfriends. The young boys will cut banana leaves, roll it into a bundle and give to his girlfriends for wrapping food items. When the sun kisses the western hills, they start climbing up the same path repeating the exchange of appreciation and stolen looks. As soon as they reach the village, they part only to meet again at the ladies' dormitories at night[6]. Tired eyes but love knows no pain and impel young hearts to forget the day's hard work. So their love affairs develop day by day till the day comes when the young man can no longer resist telling his parents to ask for the hand of the girl for marriage. When the harvest season comes, the young men are busy making baskets and other presents for their beloved ones and the girls do some extraordinary works for their lovers during the (akhu) festival season. The lovers search the hearts of each other and if their love is blessed with parental approval, the result is obvious. Sometimes the parents consult the omens whether the proposal is worth trying, and if the result is in the affirmative, well and good. The match making take place when a considerable age after puberty has been attained, the minimum marriageable age of a boy is twenty years and of a girl is sixteen years. C.R. Pawsey writes, "I cannot understand how infant marriages first arose in the naked Rengma villages unless it is the result of the nakedness. Most girls seem to marry before the age of twelve"[7]. A go-between or intermediary, preferably senior Khel woman is engaged to convey the proposal.

Normally, this woman visits the girl's house more than once in the matter[8]. Till the engagement is settled, the mediator runs from girl to girl's parents and then to the boy's parents. It is the custom of the Rengmas that the girl's family will not give a positive response on the first approach even if they wish to build family ties. In some areas, the girl's parents force their unwilling daughter to join hands with the boy accepting the wealth and the background of the boy's family. As a sign of virginity the girl keep her head shaved till engagement and when her engagement is settled, she will no more shave her hair, which is a sign of respect to her would-be husband. By seeing the hair growing on the head of an unmarried woman, people will come to know that she is engaged. According to the means of the bridegroom; fowls, dogs, spirits and spearheads are given as a present to the parents of the damsel selected, and her consent being obtained as well as her parents' (for she has a right to refuse), a grand feast is given by the bride groom on the day of his marriage to the whole village[9]. In return, they are obliged to present the newly married couple with a new house in the village. The boy's father requests an old man from the same clan to give a present to the girl's father. This old man carries a bamboo cup of azü (rice beer) and spearhead to the girl's house to present it to the girl's father[10]. He will be accompanied by some relative of the boy. The bride's mother brews the rice beer brought by the boy's party and then shares it with all the members gathered. They will drink and exchange their views about their family relation. On the third evening, the same old man will take another spearhead from the boy's father and go to the girl's father's house. This time he goes alone to present the spear-head, and inform them the date to have a family gathering to discuss about the date and other formalities of the marriage.

Except the bridegroom, all the family members and relatives will go to the girl's house where another spearhead is given to the girl's father. Relatives of both sides will discuss and fix the date for marriage. Normally the wedding is organised in winter season. In some villages, the bride's father begins by asking the price beyond the spears he had received from the boy's father if the latter happens to be a wealthy man in the village. For it is not etiquette for the parents themselves to come to a final settlement. Therefore, an experienced man who acts as an intermediary settles it. Knowing everyone on both sides well, he fixed a price which both sides accept as reasonable. The actual payment of the price is left till later, and installments are often spread over many years. To receive a marriage price for a daughter is in no way an immoral sale of the girl. The price is compensation for her leaving the clan, and is of immense moral value.

When the parties belong to different villages, the bridegroom goes to the bride's village with men of his own clan and of his mother's clan, and men who have married the women of his own clan. When all are well drunk, men of the bride's village try to seize the visitors' property, and a friendly fight takes place in which no ill will is shown. Really valuable property, such as ivory armlets, is not taken, bu t clothes and small ornaments are torn from their owners and cannot be claimed back. Indeed, it is required by custom that some property at least should be seized from their visitors. A similar fight sometimes takes place when the two parties belong to the same village, but nothing more than a cloth or two is ever taken, and it is not required by custom that anything should be taken at all. Meanwhile the bridegroom builds his house[11], and the wedding is arranged to take place before the "field clearing feast" in March, which marks the beginning of the agricultural operations for the year, and after which it is taboo to marry. After the date being fixed, the mediator goes to summon the girl and her parents to his parents' house. On the first and second night, she must refuse to go, or she will not live long. On the third night, the girl and her parents obey the summons, and both families feast together. The same feast is organised by the girl's parents and invite the boy and his parents. When the marriage week approaches, both the families start preparing drinks, food and others. The boy's parents arrange pigs, cows, chickens and even mithuns, depending on the wealth position of the boy's family. The night before the marriage ceremony, a young man from the boy's clan will be sent to invite their relatives. He will secretly go to invite the relatives of both families when everyone is in bed. He takes small pieces of banana leaves and places it in the house[12] of the relatives without informing the invitees. The leaf signifies the special invitation as well as the expectation of the gift. For those who had experienced sex wit man will have to place the banana leaf along with a little amount of salt. An ordinary invitation will be a verbal invitation and these people need not bring any present.

The ceremonial marriage of the Rengma is very simple which is organised at the bride's house in the afternoon. People, especially the old men of the two families, will bless the new couple and then drink and eat whatever is being provided to them. In return they are obliged to present the newly married couple with a new house in the village[13]. Feast may continue till dusk, and when the feast is over, they will lead the bride to her new house. The procession is thus composed: First the price decider and spear-heads presenter, next the new couple followed by bridesmaid and woman mediator, and then the relatives and family and finally a number of young people carrying the meat, presents and personal belongings of the bride etc. While proceeding to the groom's house, none of them will turn back, lest divorce in the future. It is genna for the bride's parents to accompany their daughter to her permanent home, for they believe that their daughter will not live long if they do so. In the new house, some feast and merry making takes place after which they will congratulate the new couple and return to their respective houses. For two nights the bride and bridesmaid will sleep together whereas the groom will sleep alone in the same room. The next day, they will observe house gennah (house sanctification ceremony). Early in the morning, the husband will go to the jungle and bring two twigs of *callicarpa sp.* (cchenchenga) and place then at crevices of the door. It is the tradition that when the leaves are stuck in the crevices by the side door wall, nobody will either take or get inside the house. He takes three pieces of aliphighi leaves and loosely knots one at the front wooden bar and the other two at the inner bar at the innermost room of the house. He pours ajüxhi (rice flour mixed with water) three times each on the aliphighi. Meanwhile, he utters words of prayer which read,

'Oh! Spirit God! Bless this house; grant us long life and a good relation. Bless us with many children. Shower your blessings on the house and on the field. Let there be good health and multiply our wealth. Lo! I am giving you, you eat and drink.' The bride generally does not go out of the house the next day or even the following day except for nature's call[14].

Except the husband who performs rituals, the bridesmaid does all the household work for three days. On the third evening, she will arrange the bed for the new couple and go to her house. Their marriage ceremony is not over till family gathering programme is held for which two different types of rice beer is prepared. The first type is called azzütsa (malt flour) without yeast for the family. The other beer are called azughi (beer with yeast) which is for the common people. When the beer matures, all the relatives of both sides are invited to grace the family gathering feast. Whoever comes, will bring a present to the new couple because they are short of household materials (nshü-u). The wife will give a bamboo cup of rice beer to the invitees, who will bless the new couple and drink. Whereas the new couple will drink the beer made without yeast (azzütsa). In the evening, the new couple kills a cock without any defect and then cooks it without chilly and eats. And then the marriage ceremony is considered to be over. Next, they will begin looking for the right time to prepare for the pig sacrifice ceremony.

Within a month of marriage, another simple ceremony is performed which finally separates the girl from her clan and attaches her to that of her husband, enabling her to go to his granary. This she could not do while she was in any sense a stranger. First an old man comes with two chickens, one for each couple, and sacrifices them with a prayer for good fortune. A few days later, the bride goes down to the village spring in the middle of the day, a time when she is unlikely to meet anyone there. She washes thoroughly, first her head, then her arms and then her body and legs. Finally, she holds the two bottom corners of her skirt against the upper ones and pours water into her lap. She then makes a wisp of nine kinds of twigs and waves it in the air to brush away all evils and throws it away with a prayer for health and wealth. This removes any taint of her old clan, which may have clung to her. In the Tesophenyu group, an additional ceremony is held that night to symbolise the final union of husband and wife. The girl shuts the door of her house when she comes up from the spring and kills and cooks a hen. After her meal, she goes to her bed. The husband eats a separate meal outside the closed door, with his spear and dao by his hand. He then goes in and lies down by his wife, but may not speak to her.[15]

The marriage customs of the Eastern Rengma, in most ways, differ from the proper Rengma. The marriage of children before puberty was largely practiced by the Eastern. C.R. Pawsey had clearly stated during his tour to Sohimi, one of the villages of Eastern Rengma, which read, "I cannot understand how infant marriages first occurred in these naked Rengma villages unless it is a result of the nakedness. Most girls seem to marry before the age of twelve"[16]. It is particularly common for a rich man's son to be married when he is a mere child. His father arranges it because he can afford to set up a house and property. His wife will be of the same age, the daughter of someone who is glad to take the chance of a good match. These little couples live happily, for they are children, together. Polygamy is common; a man's second marriage is always to a woman of his own choice, a widow or divorced wife. The two wives live in the same house, but the first is definitely senior. An old woman acts as a go-between, and when the marriage has been definitely arranged, the bridegroom gives five cakes of salt to the bride. This is regarded as a sign that the couple is definitely engaged. The bride's family, in return, kills a large pig and gives present of pork to the groom's family. On that day, an old woman that served as go-between, must come with the boy and drink in his future father-in-law's house. Next day, the bridegroom's family kills a pig and the bride and her family, with the old woman, comes and eats and drinks with them. Both sides present a large amount of cooked meat to the old woman. The actual marriage takes place the following cold weather, and at first the young couple does not set up a separate establishment, but lives in the bridegroom's father's house. In the Miepfuri village, mass marriage system prevails. Every year, on the last day of the (Akhu) festival, all the intending candidates get married. The night before the marriage ceremonial, the boy's parents arrange drink and meat and then send the boy to present it to his future father-in-law. He will call some friend and will go to present the bride's parents. Normally, the marriage feast was light, because in a village many get married on the same day separately and only close relatives are invited to the marriage ceremony. The bride goes to the groom's house in procession in the evening, accompanied by the girl's friends and the mediator. At the groom's house, all the women in the village join the bride in the feast in her father-in-law's house in which no man may take part. That night the husband will have to stay at another house and the bride will sleep with friends at the father-in-law's house. The next day he returns and begins normal life with his wife. About a year (or more in case of child marriage) late in the cold weather, the parents move to a new house or construct a new house for the new couple to live in. at the completion of the new house, a fowl is sacrificed, and he takes it to his wife, the couple keeping 'genna' for that day.

Divorce

Divorce, although permissible under the customary rule, is very rare. There is no ceremony connected with divorce. Incompatibility of temperament is the chief reason, but couples in areas where it is rare usually make an honest effort to get on. If a woman is divorced for adultery or blamed in some other case, her parents or other representatives have to return the marriage price. She is allowed to take her property, but the immovable property cannot be claimed. If the man is to blame, he can claim back none of the marriage price he has paid, and has no right to live with his wife in the house. He has to leave the house for his wife and the children if any. But divorce after having two or more children is very rare.

Fetish Stones

The Rengma believes that certain stones called charm stones (avüü or takvü) bring good fortune to individuals or villages. They are smooth, water-worn stones, varying in size[17] and are kept under the head-tree, foot of totem post (Agghon) of the morung (azüüghüü or rensing) or by individuals in their houses or granaries[18]. Among the Eastern Rengmas, only clans and individuals own them. One stone called Therushing, is regarded as the property of the whole tribe, as it stands close to where the original village was founded on Therügu Hill[19]. When I enquired, I was told that these stones move here and there or sometimes disappeared and heard it making sounds like a rat[20]. There is belief that it has come by itself singly or in groups to their stated places. I was told by some elders of Kandinu that several times they had seen avüü, like the shape of a pig, flying from Kijüü Hill to Khupvü-chü (beside Chunlikha Village), a place where people never cultivate because they still believe this area as the place of Satan. Another tradition says that the charm stones migrate from village to village and to husband and wife who give birth to nine or ten children[21]. These classes of stones have been handed down from generation to generation. Though luck stones, when they fail to propitiate, brings ill luck to individuals or communities as a whole, for which cocks are sacrificed to please them. The most sacred of the Tseminyu Village stone is called Takvü Kepega. It is said at night people used to see twinkling lights at zushwühwen, near an obsolete Thongsünyu village. Many people fearfully watched it, but one day, seven great warriors from Tseminyu made up their minds to go and search for it, and wanted to see what it really is. They were able to reach the right site from where they found two stones of different sizes sparkling in the river, where three small streams ran into another. These stones are considered to be husband and wife, Takvü Kepega is the husband and Takvü Kepesu is the wife named to them by the villagers. Kepesu was so large, so they could carry to their village Kepega whose size was small. Their triumph was short-lived, for, so great was the power that all these seven men lost their lives in war within a short time. The villagers kept it at the East Side of the village. Every night, the people heard the stone crying. One night a man in his dream saw Kepega crying and saying, "My wife is in the west, so take me to the west." When he narrated the matter to the village elders, they carried it to the west, kept hidden on a cliff outside the village where it still is. Thereafter it cried no more. Men who have done the head-taking ceremony, whose duty is to wash it and offer a cock sacrifice yearly at the zükulu ceremony[22], may only see it. The blood is sprinkled from its head to the bottom. Truly experienced by the village, a common person who sees it falls sick or sometimes becomes mad. From it the fortune of the village for the year can be foretold. If there are ashes on it, there will be a house burned; if a husk of paddy is on its head side, people who cultivate far distance will harvest plenty, and if it lies on the bottom side, who cultivate nearby the village will harvest plenty; if a stick or branch lies on it, someone will be killed by a fall from a tree; if there are tooth-marks on it, a tiger will claim a victim; if blood stains is found on it, someone will be killed by raid. It is said that a group of Angamis comprised of six villages and of about 300 men started a raid on Tseminyu: When they got there, seeing that the village was a large and powerful one, they said that they had come to ask their assistance in attacking Kohabama. They told the fighting men of Themokedimah (Tseminyu) to go ahead and they would follow. Shortly after they had started, the Mezoma man shut the gates of the stockade and commenced their butchery on the women and children. The Themokedimah men got notice of this and returned; finding the attacking party inside they set fire to their house[23]. The fugitives who fled in Kepega direction were saved, and the Angamis who followed became hopelessly bewildered and were killed.

The kepega stone is believed to be full of magic of great potency. Other luck stones, which are kept under the head-tree, are washed by the same person on the same day[24]. In addition, the warriors will fence the area. Among them, the first man who begins the fence will not eat rice for three days. Another famous stone called Singnyu Khandrang Tso (The stone of Kandrang the stranger) lies on the path leading from the Govt. bridle path to Tsokonkonyu, where it runs along the crest of a ridge, with a sheer cliff on one side. It is obviously a small monolith. There used to be two, mother and son, but the mother stone was thrown down the cliff about 1925 by some person unknown. The story, known even in distant Angami villages, is that a man took as wife a woman from a strange village. He treated her badly, and she ran away with her little son and died where the stone now lies. The little boy played by the dead body of his mother, and was always trying to crawl to the edge of the cliff to pluck a wonderful flower, but a gust of wind always drove him back. He would climb onto his mother's body and suck her dry breasts, but he got weaker and weaker, and when the body of the mother decayed, he was impaled on one of her ribs and died. Both were then turned to stone. A man once tried to drag them apart, but the woman appeared to him in a dream, told him her story, and sang the following song:

> Singnyu anyu nnyü
> Stranger child born
> Fpfü lo nizungcho ungwa
> Carrying lifting hilltop becoming
> Mi koho mi niyetsi pyeng kho ti
> Man even man darling separate away will be
> Tse mi kho nmuyale
> But man away unwilling
> Khasa khi sangdrümu thürüchiso
> Plains on storm is coming up.
> Niyetsi sü kebi lo phyinyiho
> Darling joining pair take have pity
> This may be freely translated:
> "I, a stranger, bore a son
> And carried him to a hilltop.
> A man tried to tear me from my darling,
> But I cannot leave him.
> Your deed will bring a storm up from the plains;
> Have pity on us and leave me with my darling[25]."

The powerful type of magic stone, called annivüü fire charm[26] is still found at Kandinu village. When enquired on how it was named so, I was told that at night it used to burn and fly over the village. In addition, time to time, this fell on the house and burned the houses. How the charm came to be there, it is not known. It is said that once there lived a good number of young men from the Wanthangza clan in the village. They were brave warriors who protected the village and fought against the enemy's raids. On seeing their village being burned several times by this magic stone, they pushed it away to the east of the village which is found in a small stream of river. Ill-fate spread in the village, soon after it was dragged out from the village. One after another who were involved in throwing away the luck stone died. This tragic incident spread like flame to distance neighbouring villages within a short interval of time. Consequently, for quite sometime, there was no visitor or guest found in Kandinu village.

Ordinary luck stones are common to all the tribes. They are small, rounddish, and black with a smooth surface. Usually only 'medicine men' know where they can be found, but occasionally ordinary people come across one in the jungle. When one is obtained, an offering is made, and the finder waits to see if the stone brings his good or bad luck. In the latter case, it is thrown away, but stones, which bring good luck, are kept in a pot in the granary[27], clan's morung, or sometimes under the village's head tree. If only one is obtained it will soon find a mate, it is believed, in some mysterious way known only to itself, and there will be two in the pot where there was only one before. These two breed[28] until there may be quite a large family. The idea that stones can breed, begetting and conceiving offspring is not easy to assimilate. If neglected, the stones fly away, and some people say they have heard them whizzing like those of rats. To keep them happy, an offering is made to them every year sometimes they are washed with clean water. All these stones were named differently and accordingly they believed. Such names are Ane-vüü (boiled rice stone), because of the food it brings to the village; Amisü-sievüü (cattle hoof stones), which increases the herds of the 'khel' to have large families; Alie-vüü (enemy's head) brings success in war. Other stones are Amie-vüü (Ancestor's stone) are kept buried in pots in the house of an old man. Clan stones and private stones, are examined and washed at the aqhu kimitha (body cleaning) ceremony, just as village stones are two kinds called Ashü-vüü (cunt charm stone) and Azzon-vüü (penis charm stones) bring children. The approaches to the stones are marked with the remnants of innumerable sacrifices of eggs, fowls and pigs at the spot are reported to stay there of their own accord. At the same time, a prayer is offered that brings prosperity to the village. The stones are said to come of their own accord at the proper date; after they have been feasted with due ceremony they are again buried privately by, old man, and his companions.

A group of stones knows to all Eastern Rengma lies just outside the Eastern Angami village of Phakekedzumi. It is believed to be the petrified trunk, arms, and legs of one Khorpu of Sahunyu who was killed long ago by raiders from Swemi. The spear wounds on the trunk are still pointed out. No one touches it, for to do so would bring on a violent storm. In this section of the tribe there are few clan and private stones, which are washed and fed when the house, in which they are kept, is rebuilt and at the annual Ngazu ceremony which marks the close of one year and the beginning of the next. At the ceremony, offering of fowl or fish, boiled rice and rice beer are made to them before the feast begins[29].

Another great magic stone called Khruokuo (stag turned into stone). A hunter from Liphori went alone for hunting animals. Luck favoured him a stag, the size of which made him need to call his friend to carry. For fear of putrefying, he cut the abdomen, pulled out the stomach and intestines, placed them nearby, and then came back home. When he went back to carry it in the morning with a party, not without surprise, he found the dead stag completely petrified, not even the intestines and stomach remained flesh. Though changed into stone, the shape and colour remained exactly as it was before. The hole of the bullet shot and the cut mark of the dao never changed. In the latter year, this stone was believed to be the rain stone. When the need of rain was felt for the crops in the field, the villagers observed a day's 'genna' and went to the place where it is laid. They cover it with any kind of leaves and offer prayers. They then return with singing and chanting. Before they reach home, the rain always pours down. Generations back, perhaps out of ignorance or conversion to a new faith, people began to disregard it and made use of it as their sharping stone. The smooth surfaces which is good to polish the flat surfaces of the blade and makes them to break it into pieces for a whetstone. In my field study, half of the body still remained below from the original place. When inquired, they said the students used it as a game, dragging it downward in order to enjoy the stone rolling down.

Notes and References

1. James Hastings, *Religion and Ethics*, p. 850.
2. Verrier Elwin, *The Nagas in the 19th Century*, 1969. p. 358.
3. Marriage between cross-clans is taken as hybrid and issue are regarded as superior. See *The Ao Naga Religion and Culture*. p. 109.
4. John Butler, *A Sketch of Assam*, 1847, p. 164.
5. Verrier Elwin, *The Nagas in the 19th Century*, p. 523.
6. The unmarried ladies sleep in a rich man's house of the village.
7. Tour Diary of D.C., Naga Hills, 1921. (Esq. M.C., T.C.S).
8. The Gazetteer of India, Nagaland, Kohima Dist. p. 79.
9. John Butler, *Travels and Adventures in the Province of Assam*, 1885 p. 124.
10. In some villages, the go-between woman does this.
11. It is not compulsory to build before marriage. Many build their own house after marriage.
12. Kept in the kitchen or at the door.

13. Verrier Elwins, *The Nagas in the 19th Century*, 1969. p. 358.
14. The Gazetteer of India, Nagaland, Tuensang District. p. 48.
15. J.P. Mills, *The Rengma Nagas*, p. 213.
16. Tour Diary of Dy. Commissioner, Naga Hills. 1921.
17. There are some large sizes.
18. See *The Lotha Nagas*, p. 166.
19. J.P. Mills, *The Rengma Nagas*, p. 229.
20. Manthi Kath of Kandinu village who performed kethi ceremonies.
21. Mr. Shüghüphen Wanth, who had performed Githie ceremony was being converted to Christianity. After his conversion to Christianity, he went to the head tree and threw away all the children, which were found under the head-tree of Kandinu village. Nevertheless, he had a dream, the spirits questioning him why he had thrown their children.
22. See Page No. 25
23. From the chief commissioner of Assam, No. 2344, dated 28th Oct. 1877, Office Note.
24. See Zükulu Ceremony, p. 24
25. J.P. Mills, *The Rengma Nagas*, pp. 230, 231.
26. House Burning Stones; See *The Ao Nagas*, p. 290.
27. Similarly among the Dusums of Borneo, curios shaped stones are placed with the unhusked rice to act as talismans. (Evans, studies in Religion, Folk-lore and Customs in British North Borneo and The Malay Peninsula. p. 31) J.P.M.
28. See *The Angami Nagas*, p. 408.
29. J.P. Mills, *The Rengma Nagas*, p. 234.

Chapter 6

Medicine Man

Medicine-men existed among the Rengmas, but were far from common. They may be of either sex and usually have epileptic tendencies. As in all Naga tribes, they combine the functions of fortune-tellers and physicians. These are the points which distinguish them from the priests, with whom they are in no wise to be confused. Their duties are different and their powers are different. A medicine man (Tamanyu or dama) will say what sacrifice is necessary in a certain case, but a priest offers it (unless of course, the offering has to be conveyed to the other world,[1] when another "medicine-man" is called in.)

Roughly speaking, the priests and the private individuals acting as priests carry on the normal religious life of the community, the medicine man being called in only to deal with the abnormal. Were sickness and sorrow to cease, the medicine man would find him out of work. They claim that their familiar spirits reveal to them in dreams which sacrifices are necessary for the recovery of a patient and they themselves will suck 'dirt' from a painful limb, producing from their mouths little stones and tufts of hair, stone or wood, or whatever is causing the pain that they have extracted. Patients are frequently treated in this way, but the practice does not seem to be nearly as common as it is among the Naga tribes. If the conditions are too stringent, the medicine man counters by saying that his familiar spirits are away and he cannot undertake the treatment. My memory is able to go back two decades back when an old man from my village was sucking out dirt from a man's head. I saw him using a stag horn sucking out the dirt-contaminated blood and on the topside of the horn being covered by tobacco leaves.

I was then, just a boy, so the reasons were not enquired. In the recent past, a famous medicine man from Tesophenyu breathed his last leaving the spirit to his son. People do not go for healing sickness alone, but also other matters like enquiring the loss of material or theft case, future life etc. Most people to whom the spirits offer their powers accept them by doing the sacrifice and refraining from forbidden food. (bamboo rats, rats and squirrels, all of which are regarded as stupid animals.), for there is a living of sorts to be made out of the trade which will last till extreme old age. When, therefore, persons of good family acquire these powers, their relations often surreptitiously mix forbidden things with their food, and so annul their powers, but make possible the continuance of their clan.

Ceremonies for Illness

A Rengma, when sick, usually attributes his illness to the malice of an evil spirit (gejong), who has either introduces some foreign matter, such as hair or a little stone, into his body or causes his soul (aghamuo) to desert him at a certain place. In certain cases, a medicine man has to be called in, who can see and "extract" any foreign body which may be the cause of the trouble, or can say at what spot his soul left him and is likely to be lurking. To enable the man to regain his soul, a soul caller is required, who must be an old man who has done social 'gennas'[2].

(a) Anti-devil Rites (Adsonghang chülagichü)

If any one is suffering from headache or fever, then it is presumed that he is afflicted by the power of devil or he could not stand the aura of devil or that he is in the spell of devil. So if anyone is suffering from headache, the first thing he has to do is to ward off the effect or influence of the devil. Moreover, in order to regain his health, someone has to perform the rites. For children, either father or mother performs the rites. It is believed and said that the devil is afraid of fire and charcoal. That if the child is sick, the mother collects three pieces of charcoal and holds a jug of water. Each charcoal will be waved around the head of the sick child, and then dropped into the jug, when the performance is over; the child is kept rested for a while and asked whether he is all right. In some cases it works, for which people have faith in this way of rite to ward off the devil and to heal the sick.

(b) Egg Offering Rites (Tero zükedi or Avüüghüü-ghaatsü Giden)

If anyone went to some place where he got sick, it is believed that the devil spirits attacked him. So someone has to be called to go (especially an old man of the clan) with the eggs wrapped in a *Thaumaloeccus Daüniellie* (chonghinga) leaf to the place the sick man had visited and offer the egg by cracking, or, in the event of any fire accident while burning the field; and when the fire becomes outrageous and may affect even the houses of the villagers then the egg is laid in front of the fire so that the god of fire may be appeared and the fire comes down to controllable limit. That is how the heat of the fire is doused.

(c) Chicken Rite (Avüüghüü-givüü or Tero Penro-kethyü)

This is another way of propitiating the spirit, when a person falls sick on visiting a bad place. It is believed that his soul has been arrested by the devil and he is at the mercy of the devil whose soul is tortured and tormented by the devil spirit. An old man or woman is called to perform rite for his safety. He will wave around the head of the sick man five or seven times with the chicken and then take it to the jungle, the place where the sick man had visited. The chicken is released in the jungle as an offering to the devil spirit and words uttered to the spirit,[3] "I have loosened the chicken, it is your turn to loosen him." He then takes his spear and jabs the butt into the ground a number of times, in order that the spirit may think that a large number of men have come to call back the sick man's soul and so be more ready to let it go.

Finally, he calls out the name of the patient several times and says, "Oh so and so! We have let a chicken go for you. Come back, come back." On his way back to the village, he must keep on calling the sick man by name, anybody who sees him on the way will have to give him side and it is taboo for the man to reply even if they speak to him. On arrival at the patient's house, he says, "I have called so and so. Has he come?" One of the inmates will answer, "He has come". Then, he says, "Close the door." And the inmates shut the door. It is genna for the rite performer to go inside the house of the sick man on this day. The next day he will visit the sick man where he will be given a drink and meat. The old man's fee for this ceremony is a basket-full of paddy[4].

Notes and References

1. J.P. Mills, See *Supra*, p. 236
2. Similar practiced by the Lothas.
3. Verrier Elwin, *The Nagas in the 19th Century*, p. 288.
4. This employment of a scapegoat chicken is common to Lothas, Aos, Semas, Changs and probably most Naga tribes.

Chapter 7

Feast of Merit

So important a part does feasts of merit play in the life of the Naga tribes and such valuable examples of Naga ceremonial at its fullest do they provide, that no picture of the tribe could claim to be completed without a full description of them. A brief description will here suffice. The series is strictly prescribed, and every man tries to proceed as far in it as his means permit, for on the feasts he has given his social status depends. It would be an unheard of thing for a man to go no further with the series if he could afford to so. It is the ambition of every man to proceed as far as he can in the series and thereby gain for himself honour both for his life and life after death, and gain for his clan and village the favour of the spirits and the prosperity of great men of the future. He wins, too, thereby the coveted right to wearing certain clothes and ornaments, lifting the apse roof of verandah higher[1] and erecting the Totem pole (aghon) in the verandah and of decorating his house in a particular way, and the skulls of the sacrificed animals hanging in the outer room bring prosperity not only to him, but to his heirs who inherit them after him. Socially and economically, the feast is very valuable. The ceremonies tend to strengthen the ties of kinship, and add their wealth in the form of rice and meat, which is distributed and shared with all, down to the very poorest. Dr. Elwin has defined, "The feast of merit, which bestowed so much distinction on their donors, showed that it was the distribution of wealth rather than its possession that was important. And this distribution included everyone, not merely one's own relation and rich friends, but the poorest and the least important." No one but a married man can give any of the feasts, for the wife plays an honourable and conspicuous part throughout. The labour entailed in collecting firewood, making rice-beer, buying animals and cutting meat, preparing food and so on is very great, and is only accomplished with the aid of eldest men of the clans who had finished the requisite series of the feast, who have special duties assigned to them through out. Besides, women too, are called to help the men until the ceremony is over. The actual act is never done by the giver of the feast, who may not even see the blow struck or taste any of the meat of the bull or mithun sacrificed[2]. The feast of merit ceremonies is so important and it differs from region to region, so I will begin with the Northern Group, taking the feasts in order.

Cock Throat Strangle (Avüüghüü Givüü)[3]

The clan will act as the priest of the giver. The giver arranges a cock without any defect and unblemished (legs and beak should be without yellow in colour), with the couple sitting inside the house an old man squats in the doorway with his stick in his left hand and a cock in his right. He clutches the legs and waves it around the couple and offers prayer for them, "Oh Spirit God! Bless this house; let there be no sickness and difficulty; may they live long; prosper their wealth at home and in the field. Let their generations spread mountains. I am sacrificing this cock for you. You bless this house" He then strangles it to death between his finger and thumb. In some houses, two fowls are sacrificed, one for the husband and one for the wife. He eats the fowl, cooked with ginger and salt alone. The woman who has been blessed goes down to the village spring and washes herself and brushes herself with a whisk made of seven or nine kinds of jungle leaves, praying as she does so that all illness and misfortune may leave her.

Ceremony for Scapegoat (Amuhu Keden)

This is another sacrificial ceremony for the sins purification of the house. Every householder must do it once, and it is often repeated if the need for it is felt. An old man (apfüwa) of the clan and the son-in-law (acüünaawa) are called and on arrival, is given a meal. Any kind of animal can be sacrificed, depending on the position of the giver (common people sacrifice piglets whereas the rich man sacrifices goat or cow). A sharpened bamboo (aghana) is then handed over to the old man on which every member of the household has dabbed some spittle, cooking pots, a small sow, rice, rice-beer and some salt mixed with pounded *Rhusemialata* (Adhama) berries.

With these they will go outside the door, which is shut vertically[4] behind him by the family, who remain inside the house and watched if they liked. Apfüwa will tie the animal with long rope and holds the rope. He then walks a few steps to the east and says, "Oh sunrise! This is a fine pig. Its feet are white. Its forehead is white. Its teeth are perfect. This is a lucky day. I am offering the pig to the spirit God. What will I do with this animal?" He then turns to the west, walks a few paces and says, "Oh Sunset! The Sunrise has told me to ask you. This is a fine pig. Its feet are white. Its forehead is white. Its teeth are perfect. This is a lucky day. What will I do with this animal? He will repeat the same three times each. These preliminaries over, he lays the rope on the ground on his right side and squats by it. He points the pig with the bamboo in various parts of the body saying, "No, this will pierce the nose. No, this will pierce the eye. No, this will pierce the liver," and so on. Finally, he points it over the heart and says, "Oh! They have compromised. With one mind I will kill," and drives the bamboo in with the words "This is where our ancestors pierced pigs." He then lights a fire with a fire thong and singes the pigs. When the meat is cut, he sprinkles the blood three times to the right and three times to the left with the words, "Oh spirit! I make offering to you first." The meat is cut and hung in the front of the house. A piece of rib is placed on the two-foot bamboo. He will chop it and push towards the outskirts of the village saying ayajü, ayajü. In the meanwhile, acüüanawa will guard the meat from being eaten by dogs. The rib and bamboo will be pushed out of the village and thrown away. For they believed that the sin of the house had been chopped into pieces and then cast out from the house. They will cut the meat into about an inch square size, and three pieces are pierced in a bamboo rope, which is hung on the front house of the eldest man of each clan in the village. The remaining meat is distributed between the two and taken home. For three days, the inmates of the giver will not go to the place where the ribs and the bamboo are thrown. Failing to comply, the bad spirits will return home.

Pig Sacrifice (Avü Kechüna)

This is the most common and important religious ceremony observed by the Rengma people. Even the poorest of the poor in the village must observe at least once in the lifetime. This can be observed repeatedly at any occasion, even in the midst of other religious ceremonies if the need is felt. The main purpose of this sacrificial ceremony is to appease God and in return to receive blessing for physical well being and prosperity of life. The actual ceremony lasts for a day. Whenever the couple made up their minds to observe this ceremony, the husband will inform his intimate friend[5], who goes to collect the required materials and carry it to his own house, and then keeps it at his house. At dusk apfüwa will come to carry it to the giver's house who will act as a priest. He will calls one more boy (any one of the in-law's son) to assist the apfüwa who is called 'Acüünawa'.

Preparation of azü, ajüxhi and others start three days ahead of the main day. In every ceremony pouring of ajüxhi[6] is strictly practiced, without which the ceremony is considered as incomplete. The pouring of ajüxhi signify the sanctification act of the inmate and whatever is inside the house. A day before the ceremony, he entrusts the in-law, may-be the father of acüünawa to go for collecting ashüshü (reed) three segments long, *Musa sumatrama* leaf(Anga) *thaumaloeccus daniellie* leaf (chonghinga) from the jungle. The in-law goes to collect the required materials and carry it straight to his house, and then, at dust apfüwa will come and carry it to the host house where he will be joined by achüünawa. The two are welcomed very warmly by the host family and they are given the ceremonial rice beer. As usual apfüwa offers prayer and blow off the top layer of the rice-beer in his leaf cup, and thereafter drinks. Apfüwa makes bamboo poker and bamboo knife (Aghana)[7] for killing and cutting the pig respectively. He will take three segments long bambusa which was brought by the in-law of the host and make the scratch marks on each sigment; nine on the top sigment, three in the middle and nine on the bottom segment; three twigs of *Musa sumatrama* are over-lapped and tears it half at two sides, making it into nine pieces,[8] which bends down when it is rolled over the top sigment and is bound it with the bambusa thread[9]. The same number of twigs is torn and bound at the middle and the bottom segment. The top most portions are forked with two tip points for piercing the pig lever. A new hearth is also made, having three stones. Then a salt is put on one stone, a lump of ginger on the other, and a handful of mald paddy on the last stone. This new hearth is made mainly for the religious ceremonial purposes and can be used hereafter. When the preparation is completed, apfüwa and acüünawa will stand opposite to each other and then the host of the pig sacrifice will give a handful of salt to the former and a lump of ginger to the latter not forgetting to remind them to abstain from sexual act till the ceremony is over. As soon as they leave the house, the wife will close the door and start pounding the malt for ajüxhi.

Early in the morning before the second crow of the fowls apfüwa and acüünawa will come to the host house for the main ceremony of the day. Before doing any work, apfüwa wears xhikhathsü (traditional shawl worn by the common people). Two corners of the shawl are loosely knotted round the right shoulder, and the other two side is twisted across the back body and then lashing it around the left shoulder: The fold is used as a pouch or a bag[10]. When the shawl is worn, they go out to kill the pig; with bamboo poke the pig is prod to dead. It is singed and cleaned with water and cut with the newly made bamboo knife. Unlike Amuhu Giden ceremony, the meat is taken inside the house. A portion of lever is sliced out and then chopped into six small pieces of a half inch square size, and another piece of about two inches square. Achünawa hands over the three segments long bambusa to apfüwa, which was prepared the previous night. He pierces three pieces each on the two points and covers the two points as a lid with the larger piece of liver[11]. This complete set is called Chokha Gighie. Apfüwa climbs on the beam and binds it at the front-post inside the house. Meanwhile achüünawa will give light to him by burning the dry reeds, because this is done before dawn, if any mistake is made while binding it (leave folded, torn etc) the host will immediately fall sick, such as with fever, headache or stomach pain. As and when the mistake is checked and corrected, the giver will become alright. If the binding is completed acüünawa passes him ajüxhi (flour mixed with water) who pours it at achüü (leaves bound at ghokha).

When the offering of the giver to the spirit God, and the sanctification act is over he will come down and make new mug with a gourd. Everyone will go inside the inner most room. Apfüwa makes the fire on the new hearth and then cooks a handful of rice in an earthen pot. When the rice starts boiling apfüwa will hold the leaf cup (achü-nkhi) and stand nearby the wooden vat (apfüqhu) filled with complete set of kitchen utensils,[12] acüünawa also holds a leaf cup and stands nearby the main post of the house. Here, the giver draws the water from the boiling pot with the new mug and then pours it six times alternately into the cups of apfüwa and acüünawa. Again apfüwa will cook only three pieces of rice in the same pot which is called 'atha ginie'. As the rice starts boiling all the family members along with the priest and others stand in queue, from the host husband, wife and then the eldest child and so on to the acüünawa the last. The giver will steer the pot with wooden spoon, tips the spoon with his forefinger, and presses on the forehead of the members starting from self to the last one three times round. When the rites are over three different types of curry is cooked by apfüwa and acüünawa. The lung is then cut into sixteen pieces and cooked with ginger, salt and *Rhusemialata* (athama), and it is shared between apfüwa (nine pieces) and acüünawa (seven pieces). As a sign of heartfelt relation between the host and apfüwa, the heart is given to apfüwa by the host. The rest of the digestive portion, like intestines, pancreas, stomach, remaining lever etc. is cooked for the open door feast.

When the curry is finished cooking, acüünawa closes the door horizontally and goes to call the eldest man of each of the clan for the open door feast. Meanwhile apfüwa cooks other curry for the common people. All the invitees will be allowed to sit in front of the house, when all of them have received their shares they offer prayer before they eat and drink. The common words of prayer run as follows: "I honour the sprit Lord of this house. Grant them health and wealth, let their children increase like the eggs of the spider". After the feast, the door is fully open and the inmates who were confined inside the house, come out to meet the old men who came for the open door feast. The messenger (acüünawa) again goes to call all the men in the village for the feast. When everyone finished coming they all shout (Keqaa) in sequence three times each, beginning and the apfüwa will eat or drink the common share. About an inch square size meat is given to every household in the village. Another five pieces of meat are pierced together with the bambusa robe and given to all close relatives of both sides, who in return, give them salt, basket of vegetables from the eldest to the youngest except the messenger, none of the inmates or any other that they wished to give. This is called awen gipha-shüü. In respect of the eldest men of each of the clan, the brain, the nose, the ears, the tongue and the deaphrone are chopped together and wrapped in the leaves according to the number of the men. The messenger then, takes it to every house and places it on the carcass at the cable. The head of the pig is cut into twelve pieces and shared between the two, apfüwa gets seven pieces where as acüünawa who gets five pieces is called Aponchen. All the waste is collected and thrown on the gulf or carried home their share, who again shares it with their close neighbour[13] or hung from the peepal tree. When all the work is over apfüwa unties the cloth which he had worn before the work began for the ceremony. It is shaken over the wooden vat, for they believe that the blessings of the people were in the pouch of the cloth worn by him. The giver kills a cock and cooks it with *Rhusemailata* berries, ginger and salt for the dinner. The family eats the chicken curry where as the two guests eat the pork curry. After the dinner they carry home their share and again shares with close nieghbours.

Old Men's Feast (Keqhai Gemishu)

A man does not ordinarily give this feast until he has accumulated wealth in the form of rice and pigs. This ceremony is to feed the old men in the village, with an aim to get their blessings. This is the first religious ceremonial step towards the social status in the society. The preparation begins by brewing three different types of rice-beer, viz, common rice-beer (Githang zü), old men's rice-beer (Giqhai zü) and the family rice-beer (Athighie zü), and at least a cow and a pig or more is required depending on the number of the population in the village. Here, an old man who had done the higher series of the feast of merit is called to act as the priest or may be apfüwa performs if he had acquired the degree. Like the pig sacrifice, acüünawa is required in this feast to assist the priest. At the preliminary function the pig sacrifice is first performed, thenceforward, the main ceremony continues. Early in the morning the eldest man comes to the giver's house, blesses the house and opens all the rice-beer pots, and then tests it. Thereafter, the host pours ajuxhi on the *callicarpa* leaves which is bound at one of the middle room beams. This is an act of sanctification of the house. During the day, all the menfolk of the village will be feasted with three pieces of meat and rice-beer. Till the feast is completed none or the inmates along with the workers will drink nor eat anything. At dusk the giver is invited by his intimate friend for smoking and drinking the rice beer, made without yeast. As a sign of purity and honour the fire is first made and then given, the smoking pipe made of bamboo and the rice beer to him for smoking and drinking. In the evening all the old men come carrying a gourd cup in their respective baskets to the host house for the old men's feast. The eldest of each clan is given first to drink who will offer prayer each clan is given first to drink who will offer prayer and blow off the top layer of their cup to god. And drink. Nine pieces of meat is shared to all with plenty rice beer. The feast continues till late night with stories and singing. At departure, their cup is filled with beer and three pieces of meat wrapped in the leaves is distributed to everyone. As a sign of showering blessing on the house each of them blow of their cup little on the ground and carry it home in their basket. After the completion of ceremonial rites and rituals, on the third day, the host will invite free labour from among the villagers to work in his field. In return, for their free labour he feeds them a splendid feast in the midst of the day work.[14]

(Ajigisa) Beginning Sacrifice

Before passing on to the beginning sacrifice, an old men's ceremony has to perform three times without which one cannot step into this ceremony. This feast is given in the winter season, usually after two or three years of the last feast. Ajigisa feast is organized twice, once for the husband and the other for the wife, which takes 16 (sixteen) days[15]. The wife either can give her feast the same year or can wait, if it is desired and rich enough to host two in a year. The main purpose of performing this ceremony is to feast the villagers and to have merry making. As being discussed, people always try to expose their wealth for fame as well as for the religious code. As such only, few rich people in the society obtain the feast of merit title. The duration of the ceremony is long, for which hectic and intensive preparation is required. The women of the giver's clan will come to dry paddy one day, and may be another evening pounding takes place.

Some of the relatives provide a basket of firewood to the host. He requires three old men of any clan who had already performed the higher series. These priests need helpers, consisting of a woman, two young boys and two young girls. The priest and the helpers are called Aghamu. They have to wear new clothes. The ceremonial feast is given on an alternate day.

First Day — Two types of rice-beer is brewed; the main rice-beer with yeast (azüghi) for the common people and the rice-beer made without yeast (azütsa) for the inmates.

Third Day — Animals are killed on this day and arranged for the rest of the other days. One of the cows must be without blemish. This particular meat is divided among the men who had already performed ajigisa upwards. All the inmates, priest and the workers will have to remain chaste and fast until the preparation is completed. The giver will abstain from eating the cooked rice and the chilli until the ceremony is over. He eats no common meat, hence, a large portion of pork meat is sliced and kept it for the host who will eat it with azütsa till the ceremony is completed. In the evening the feast begins with the game, the steaks are spread on the basket (amaxha) and displayed on the verandah. All the young men will be invited to compete. The competition starts with pushing and pulling each other making the camp lively and more fun. People who witness enjoy the game.

Fifth Day — The young men were sent to collect the *thaumaloeccus daniellie* leaves (chonghi-nga). In the mean time the priests makes the Achüüno gishon. Two bamboo posts about four feet high are erected at a distance of four feet, and in between seven pieces of reeds (achüüno) are set up in line; each top edge is cut sharp[16]. Another bamboo having three segments long is laid over the reeds on the two bamboo posts.

On each segment a piece of *musa sumatrama* leaf is lashed with aliphighi rope. The senior most priest pours ajüxhi on the leaves three times round. When the young men bring the *thaumaloeccus daniellie* leaves, it is spread on the paddy mat and select the best thirty pieces and then roll it. The eldest among them cuts the bottom side at once not leaving a piece uncut. It is untied and laid equally on three places with its tip opposite to each other. Three of the priests take one each and take it home on the last day of the ceremony. In the afternoon, the giver and his wife wrap their own share of eleven and nine pieces of meat respectively in the *thaumaloeccus daniellie* leaves. They take their own share along with the honeycomb[17] to the house of the eldest man and present it to the couple. All the male members go out to catch any puppy without a spot and defect for sacrifice[18]. It was the cultural practice that any puppy can be killed for religious ceremony without prior information or permission from the owner. One man holds the head and the other man holds the tail and then the eldest man equally cuts the middle into two portions with the bamboo knife. The eldest takes it home for eating. In the evening when the people start coming for the feast, two women dressed in complete traditional dresses come to the host house carrying their gourd cup in their respective baskets. They will pound nine holes of malt paddy with prayer, "From last year to this year I am living healthy, so I am happy. Oh! Bless this house and enrich their wealth. Let their children increase like the ants. Protect them from sickness". The two women will have to pound at the time, and any mistakes they made are laughed at by the people standing around. More over they act funny things and allow the people to laugh at them. They are lavishly fed with drink, meat and rice; besides their cup filled with the rice-beer and nine pieces of meat wrapped in leaf is allowed to carry home. In a big wooden bowl a large quantity of cooked meat is put and the young men compete eating it. This competition entertains the guest. When the feast is over eleven pieces of meat are shared among all the priests and the helpers. A big slice of uncooked meat is roasted and eaten by the three priests with drinks.

Seventh Day — The ceremonial act is almost same as the fifth day ceremony. Another seven more wooden-vats of rice-beer are brewed for the remaining days. Two sons of all the Githie in the village are invited for the feast. Everyone is given eleven pieces of meat to eat and rice beer to drink. When they get drunk the giver pours the rice beer on them; this is called aghasuo cükha kemishu (blessing foot-print feast). The priest gives a small slice of cow skin along with a cup of azütsa to the host. He drinks the rice beer but returns the cow skin. This is called aghanie giniechiwen (following the sun curry).

Ninth day — A cock without any defect is sacrificed for all the persons working at the host house as a priest and a helper. It is atonement of fault, and to propitiate God for good life. At the time of sacrifice, everyone stands in front of the house. The eldest priest holds a stick in his right hand and a cock in left; he beats the cock to squeak and waves round three times. He calls out the name of nine villages, surrounding his village (may be enemies' villages). And then utters the following words: "supon, supon khütsa khüjü, tsentsa tsenjü gitenwa hiewie gholo. "(Shortage, shortage, beg-eater, beg-drinker, bitter, sucker, extort-eater extort-drinker fellow, come here). He allows squealing and then kills it. He goes home with the cock where it is cooked and eaten. In the evening, a feast is given to the villagers.

Eleventh Day — Rest day.

Thirteenth Day — This day too a cock is sacrificed for the family members. The senior most priest performs the ceremony. He waves round the cock three times with prayer, seeking the blessings upon the house. The cock is killed and taken it home to eat. As usual, a feast is given to the public in the evening.

Fourteenth Day — The giver calls every household of the village to contribute one day's free labour. In return, he arranges a heavy lunch. The night before the working day, the giver sends a messenger (nihluwa) to all the houses informing them to come to the giver's field the next day. It is the cultural practices of the Rengmas that the messenger has to hold a *bambusa* rope, and when he enters any house and passes the information he folds the rope once. In such way, the total number of members called is known through the rope folded, and reported to the host for the necessary arrangement. On the main day the messenger will once again go round to call the houses he had entered the previous night, and call them to come for the drink with the meat before they go to the giver's field. It is not compulsory, but those who wish to eat and drink come for it. Except unavoidable circumstances, none of them fails to respond to the call; after a half-day worked a great feast is given to the people. For the whole day, the hosts will neither eat nor drink anything. Only in the evening, his intimate friend (apfüwa) calls him to his house for drinks and meat. These two men eat the pork meat with the rice beer made without yeast and smoke the beri through the bamboo pipe. He will not eat anything more at his house that evening.

Fifteenth Day — The inmates observe strict fasting. Even their animals are not fed and no outsider is entertained.

Sixteenth Day — From this day onward he can eat the chilli which is given up during the ceremony. He is also entitled to work as a helper at the Githie ceremony in other's house.[19]

Real Feast of Merit (Githie)

This is one of the greatest as well as the hardest ceremony, taking twenty-one days to complete in winter season. Only those who had finished Aji sacrifice twice can initiate the real feast of merit. The norms of the religious feast are strictly maintained, violation of it is a great offence to both the individual and the community. The preparation is the same as the precedent ceremony; firewood, leaves, bambusa, water, drying of the paddy and pounding, and others are arranged. Without having proper knowledge one can not act as one's own priest. In the great religious ceremony like the feast of merit, at least three special priests are required. Hence, he calls three old priests, one woman, two youth, and two girls as ceremonial workers. The eldest priest, in the village, whose help is unavoidable in the higher series, is called annunen. All of them have to stay and sleep in the host's house until the ceremony is completed. Like the beginning sacrifice, all the important celebrations are done on alternate days, and the other days they rest to arrange the necessities for the next day. Some days before the ceremony, his wife prepares about five pots of rice-beer for the first day ceremony.

First Day — Early in the morning before any work begins the giver will sanctify the house by pouring the Ajüxhi on the leaf bound at one of the beams in the middle room. When the eldest man blesses and has drunk the rice beer of the ceremony the rest of the men-folk are invited to drink. No meat is served on this day.

Third Day — Rest and preparation.

Fifth Day — This is the accustomed of the eldest man to offer the dough of the rice-beer and prayer to the spirit God before any work begin. It has also become the custom for him to drink before any person has touched it. A good number of animals are killed[20], and one of the unblemished cows must be killed separately. The meat is sliced and distributed to every house in the village, out of it nine sliced pieces are given to the eldest men of each clan. Three mortar or pounding tables, having three holes each is placed at the right place for the ceremony. A new fountain is made for the cleaning ceremony on the last day. In the evening, a grand feast is given to the whole village.

Seventh Day — It is considered the day of making the leaf cup and the plate (Akhishon gimkhi) and feeding the sons of the real feast of merit sacrifice (Gigici). For making the cups and the plates, the workers get eleven pieces of cooked meat. Like the Aji ceremony, a messenger is sent to call two sons of all the githie in the village for feast. As and when the invitees finished their feast, their respective cups are filled with rice beer and put pieces of meat. Everyone takes it home and when it is finished the empty cups and plates must be put in the crevices of the house wall. The rest of the ceremony is the same as the seventh day ceremony of ajigisa ceremony[21].

Eight Day — About ten to fifteen persons were sent out to catch aghamu fish alive. They will not return till they have caught the particular fish.

Ninth Day — Aghamu fish is cooked with rice and then wrapped in three or four twigs of *thaumaloccus daniellie* plant. It is placed at the leg of apfüqhu (blessing vats)[22], rice beer vat and in the granary.

Eleventh day — Pig Sacrifice.[23]

Thirteenth Day — About fifteen vats of rice beer are prepared for the bonfire ceremony. In the evening, all the men folk are invited for the feast. As they sit around the fire, cups of rice beer and plates of meat are served. They sing a song called dsiho, which goes oh....ho... in two groups.

Except anunen who stay back to perform ritual for the next ceremony, the rest of the priest and helpers go home and return the next day.

Fifteenth Day — The ceremony is notable for the stamping out of a bonfire by the young bucks of the village. The workers and the relatives arrange the firewood, water, and others and when their job is finished, the oldest priest will distribute a thick slice of meat to everyone who worked on that day. He will put three pieces of meat each with ginger and honeycomb on the *thaumaloccus daniellie* leaves which is left at three places. It is enwrapped and put in a basket, then it is hung on the roof. This is called Anuokhou-wen ssajüü. At dusk one of the old men who is going to help in the giver's house shouts, "one of the men of your khel is giving a feast. Come and feast."

All the menfold, gathered at the giver's Khel morung (azüüghüü), will come with singing dsiho song led by the eldest man. Meanwhile, workers and the relatives will be busy making the fire with *rhusemialata* wood, which crakes loudly and burns high. This is the most important game in the feast of merit, where women and children too come to watch and enjoy the feast. The men folk will put off the fire whereas the workers and the relatives will prevent it by putting more and more wood in the fire. It is bad omen to let the fire being put off. As the eldest priest stands at the veranda with a bamboo stick, the menfolk will circle round the fire. He walks round the fire three times. After first round he utters, "*Thuwana hapang he chensha ssenuo hangdenkhe*" (who ever slaps the mouth of the giver and live), and then smashes the fire with the stick. He rounds the second time and utters "*Thuwana hapan ha chesha senuo hangkhe, maqhu yalla awheentsa tie hangtsüna* (who ever slap the host mouth and live, let his body live like the sieve; he then smash the fire.

After the third round he curses the unknown man, "*Bvüsshü, bvüsshü nuo hanglo*" (may your body swell and live). Again he smash the fire and goes inside the house; there he covers his face with shawl (allonthsü) and comes out. Without a word he walks round the fire three times and lifts up the fire with his stick. Thereafter the stamping of fire begins. Those who are snatching the fire are blocked and pushed back by the helper of the giver. It is a fact that even if they held the fire or jump into the burning flame no accident is faced. When the fire-game is over limitless drink along with eleven pieces of meat is distributed to everyone who came to play and witness the game. It is genna to take home any left over. When the dawn comes on the 16th day, the workers and the relatives go out to search the firewood, which was thrown by the fire-game players. For they believed that if any wood is missed in collection, it is a bad omen for the host.

Sixteenth Day — The highest priest calls the young boys to come for the feast and spearing the effigy of an enemy. Before they come, the workers make the wooden spears and the effigy out-side the village. When the young boys come a spear is given to everyone of them, and the high priest leads them to the place where an effigy is being made. He instructs the boys to spear the effigy with the words, "Die, we are spearing you".

The Australian black fellow who works magic against his enemies by pointing and stabbing with his spear says, "Strike! Kill![24]. Colonel Shakespeare report that Kabuls too put up the effigy of a man outside the village gate and throw spears at it[25].

All the boys will again come to the host house and enjoy a splendid feast. Eighteen of them are selected to pound the paddy. In each hole, two boys pound together and while they are pounding joyfully with singing the priest will pour the water at them in order to make the feast lively. Each the pounder is given an extra meat and rice beer to take it home. When the feast is over the senior most priest sacrifices a cock for the house. The cock should be without any defect: its crest must be red, its claws should be equal in size, and its tail must be equal in length, etc. The cock is held in his right hand, and a stick in his left and he goes in-front of the house. He names eleven neighboring villages; after calling every two villages the cock is waved round once and beats it. He utters "*Supon, supon sagitenwa haawie gholo. Ghashenen dsagithan machenpfüü khütsa khüjjü gitenwa haawie gholo. Tsentsa tsenjjü gitenwa haawie gholo.* After completing the round while repeating the same words, he kills the cock and says, "The entire bad thing had been carried by you. There is no more sickness and enemy's raid. You have borne it". He takes the cock home.

The youth and the old men will come for an over-night party (benthang). In order to let everyone get drunk, the host sometimes puts the tobacco in the rice beer, without the knowledge of the drinker. The helper keeps on watching the cup and does not allow the cup to be emptied. They sing ho... ho... (qhai) three times and then sing the following song with two groups in harmony. Here, I have given only soprano part:

1. : - / s. l : s.f | m : - / m : - | d. m : s. f / m : - |
   oh! Imi kadiwa oh ilasila - wa.
2. m : - / d. r : d. r | d. r : d. r / d. r : d. r |
   Oh ! dapvü dana chana aqhai mighi whalo. Ao... Ah.. Oh....Hi...
3. Groups in cannon
   m. m : d / m. m : s. d. d I m. m : d. d. d / m. m : |
   Ao... ah.
   Worona woro yikina woro yinkina woro

m. m : s. d / m. m : d. d | l, : - /
woro yenki worotsanayi oh.. hi.

4. d'. d' : d' / l : l. s : | m : m. d / m : -| m. s : l. s / m : m. d | m : - /
chulighi thonyi mayi gha ija ghie ma jen gha Ao ah o hi.

Unison

5. s. l : d'. l /-. l. d' | l. l : - / s. l : s | m (.s : s (. f / m. s : s (. m |
Echükena epi thoro ao ai Iya ghi lo iya milo Ao ah o hi.

6. s. m : s. s / - :m. d | m : - / s. m : s.s | - :m. s / l. s: - : s. m : s / - :
O amisu kemiya o amisu kemiyao o aju
l. s : m. | s. m : s / l. d' : s | l. d' : l / s. l : s |
kepi oh oh a-ju kepi oh kepi wa eloqhai Ao ah oh hi.

Group Start

7. d'.d' : d'. l / s. l : d'. l |s. l : s. m / d ; d | s : s.l / s.s : m.m | d : d / -
Chunlighina qhachu wisha masi jensha cheche O masi kugha heghe cheche.

8. d'. d' : d' / l : l. s | m : :m.d / m : - | s : s. m / s.l : l. s | m.d / m : -
Moyonghi ma ye pvu maye ya oh maye yale kasuthonpenle Oh Hi

9. : d'. l / s.l.m :-. | l : s.l / s. l : s. l | s l : s. l / s : - : l : s. t |
oh shuli kahao oh mesu maye ao ai ao a-i Oh! Naghi O Hi

10. l : s. m / f .s l : l | s. m : s. l / s. m : d |
    Oh khetson tshuli o mari thuna gwamale. Ao ah oh hi
11. s. l : d'. l / d'. l : s | s. l : d'. m' / d'. l : s | d : d' : d'/ l. l : l | s. t :
    Itso hina pemegheb Itso hi-na pemeghe ghaton-lo ghatonlo naghi A.O.hi
12. d'. d' : d' / l. l : l | 2 times |
    ghatonlo ghatonlo   Ao ah oh hi.
13. s. m : s / m. d : m | 2 times |
    Henjülo henjülo   Ao ah oh hi.
14. s. l : d'. l / - : d'. l | s. m : - /
    Inokhu-le Inokhu-le   Ao ah oh hi.
15. s. s : s / m. d : m |
    Ghatsalo ghajülo   Ah ah oh hi.
16. s. l : s / m. d : m |
    Ghatsalo ghajülo   Ah ah oh hi.
17. s. l : f.m.m / s. l : - | m. m : d.d / m. m : d. l, |
    Süchi sanchilo süchi   worotsana woro naqhai,

After the song is sung, rice beer and meat are lavishly supplied, and when everyone get drunk, the host goes for fetching the water from the new fountain. The host runs home with the water in order to reach before any of the guest leaves the house, because it was believed that if any of them leaves while he is out, the blessing of the house go with the escapee.

Seventeenth Day — All the priests and helpers disperse for home after having feast with the host family. About a kilogram of uncooked meat and a gourd killed with the rice beer is given to all of them. They go home one by one from the eldest to the two youngest girls.

Eighteenth Day — All the inmates observe fasting.

Nineteenth Day — Cock Sacrifice[26].

Twentieth Day — The giver and his wife are ordained to wear a special shawl called allonthsü or githie-thsü. The senior most priests come to the giver's house and bless them. He holds the shawl and asks the couple to stand and then offer prayer. "May you become like banyan and ficus tree (allahu & anie). May your generation increase like the fruits of Banyan and fichus! How beautiful and handsome are you to wear these prestigious shawls" He then put the shawls on their shoulders to wear. Thereafter, he is entitled to wear allothsü shawl which common people do not even touch.

Twenty First Day — One-day free labour from every household is called to work at his field. In return, he lavishly feed them with rice, meat, and rice beer. All those who have worked at the giver's house will join the giver for not eating and drinking anything till the work is finished on that day. The host and his family members go to his special friend's house on being invited by the latter. They will smoke and drink the rice beer made without yeast. The completion of the githie ceremony entitles him to put the horn of the sacrificed cow on the gable, and the veranda apse lifted higher; each one of which represents a cow sacrifice which is highly recognized and regarded in the community.[27]

New Cow Sacrifice (Githüghüü Giyathi)

A man who is going to give the feast announces his intention after getting instruction from the eldest for the new cow sacrifice. In the mid summer when the paddy is in the ear, a Mithun is killed and distributed to his friends and relations, who all give him rice beer in return. He may not eat this mithun meat. The ceremony is held in the cold season. When the time approaches he will select his in-laws and some expert to find an unblemished cow red or white in colour from outside (Specially Lotha). It takes seventeen days to complete, and begins only on when the moon comes in the middle or becomes full moon of the month. Like the Kethie ceremony, the preparation begins by drying the paddy. It is taboo to let the fire get off the night before the paddy is dried. Early in the morning the wife will put a handful of ash in a basket and carry it to the granary. She sprays the ash on the paddy in the granary and then fills her basket full of paddy and carries it home. It is Genna to speak to any person on her even if they speak to her. Some other day a messenger is sent to inform the youth to pound the paddy. For the ceremonial act three priests along with one old woman, two young boys and two young girls are required. The procedure of the rites and ritual is almost the same as the githie sacrifice. The ceremony begins by brewing thirty to forty vat of rice beer. A good number of pigs and cows are killed and a slice of meat is distributed to the household. However, for the actual sacrifice a newly bought she cow is used. It is tied to the side post of the granary of the host in clusters on the outskirts of the village[28].

The senior most priest will hold a bamboo spear, its tip covered with a lump of ginger. He will go round the cow with words of prayer "This is a new she cow brought from other nation. I am sacrificing this to the God of creator, so may there be no sickness. May his granary and life-stock increase abundantly! Let his generation multiply like the fruits of fichus and Banyan." On after odd number of going round the cow he will spear the cow, but without any intention to kill only after the sixteenth round, he spears it to death. He makes an incision with a bamboo knife and pulls out the pancreas of which he offers little scraps to the spirit. It is chopped into small pieces and than divide it into three portions. Each portion is wrapped separately in a leaf with *Rhusemailata* berries (athama) ginger and than hung on the cable of the host house as an offering to the spirit God. The rest of the digestive system is than pull through the incision, and the young men mostly poor, fight for them, while the giver pours water over them. The carcass is fetched in front of the host house and its meat distributed among the priests and old men in the village. Here, the giver and his wife drink rice beer made without yeast and eat pork for five days, fish for five days, bamboo rat (ahiefüü) for five days and birds for one days. All this is arranged by some selected men. In return of their gift the giver gives them a sliced of meat.

On the last day, the senior most Priest carries a basket filled with implements and in his right hand holds a rob tied to the neck of a dog and will walk round the whole village with shouts:

> Who ever opposed the host let him live like this dog.
> Who ever do not follow the host word let him live like this dog.
> Who ever drink or eat before the host drink or eat will live like this dog.
> Who ever work ahead of the host let him live like this dog?

The dog is sacrificed for sanctification of the giver house. The performer takes the dog home for eating. In the evening when all the priests and worker have left for home he will cook rice and rost the meat on the newly earth and eat it.

The host did not eat the granary where the cow was tied and sacrificed. It is used for charity purposes. The grain/ paddy is distributed to the needy such as paralysed, blind, old and poor orphan people. It is also Genna to keep the granary emptied. There is some movable property restricted to be inherited by the King men as follows:

Spoon, plates, bed, clothes, and other house hold materials. Even the house can not be repaired after the death.

He is entitled to put human face carved wood on the top of the front house. He is also entitled to wear a shawl (Allonthsü) embroidered in a zigzag pattern in red colour on the two middle white bands! People pay great respect to new cow sacrifice. It is a belief that if any mistake occurs before him the germs of the new cow sacrificed by him may kill the wrong doer. People never quarrel with people, primarily because everyone has eaten his wealth

Mithun Sacrifice (Asie Giyathi)

This is the supreme sacrifice, which is the last, and the greatest sacrificial ceremony ever performed by the Rengmas. The preliminaries are the same as those in the last new cow sacrifice, up to the point when mithun is killed the previous summer. When the celebration season comes, he will request his in-laws to search for a mithun without blemish. It must have no teeth missing, no chips of the horns, no white blotch anywhere, and no whorls of hair except on the back of the neck and behind the ears. The mithun is tied at the adoncen wooden in front of the host house made by the eldest among the priests. It is kept starving for three days, for it is believed that if this be done it will fight more desperately and give better report when it is dragged around the village. On the morning of the day on which it is to be sacrificed, it is tied up in front of the Azüüghüü (morung). The giver's clansmen will tie the mithun at its horns with two ropes one cane rope and one sword-bean creeper. These two ropes are to pull forwards in the right and before while the other rope tied to the leg is to hold or pull back if the mithun become uncontrollable. The host clan pours a leaf of rice beer on its head and says, "I am sorry for you. We cannot give you jungle leaves today". It is then brought to the host house and tied to a forked post. The owner hands a leaf of rice beer to an old man of his clan. Who stands in front of the mithun and, after uttering the standard blessing addresses it as follows. "You must not injure people. Everyone has come to look at you because you are so beautiful. Go in peace and return to this house". He then pours the rice beer over the mithun, and the young men, all in full dress get hold of the ropes and drag the animal all round the village. While the mithun is being dragged round the village, it is a common practice for people to pour water on it and ask it for blessing. When it has been brought back, it is again tied to the forked post and then killed with horrible cruelty. There the best or intimate friend (apfüwa) spears it, having put more pieces of ginger and nine leaves of *ficus* on his spear and holding a corner of his cloth screening his face for shame. If the stab is not fatal, he steps away through the circle gathering of villagers who are standing and singing round the sacrifice, and hides behind the house. In a minute he returns and spears it again. When the mithun is dead, he slashes the stomach open and cuts off a little of the liver. Having ascertained from its appearance what the omens are, he chops it up into tiny pieces for the spirits. These little bits he wraps in a leaf, which he ties to the front of the house, leaving one small piece on the ground "for the hornets". The triple collar sword bean creeper that was round the neck of the mithun is hung upon the forked post. The usual fight for the intestines then takes place, and the guests drink and sing at the host house till the morning. The sacrificial meat is distributed to the poor people (miyas), and he keeps the skull and shoulder blades of the mithun in front post of the house. Other mithun, pigs and cows are killed for feast which require sixteen days to complete the ceremony. The whole village is feasted and the meat divided at the last ceremony.

A man who has given this feast earns full ornaments and cloths, and the right to lift the apse roof of verandah higher, erecting the totem pole and horns on the porch of his house.

The mithun sacrifice can be repeated often as a man can afford to do so, and at the second and subsequent ceremonies the young men taking part wear the traditional dress and horn-bit feathers in honour of the host.

Within ten days, just after the feast he organises three times free labour work on his field. Firstly, he calls only the male folk to his jhum field. On the working day early in the morning the eldest man of the host clan carries the cock and a leaf wrapped with salt, ginger and *rhusemialata* berries to the giver's field before any worker reaches the field. The cock is tied to the post at the upper edge of the field. The wrapped bundle is also hung on the same post. As well known to everyone, when all the workers reach the field they will keep their implements and march to the opposite side of the cock. They stand in straight line and wait for the signal from the old man to compete for the cock. As and when the old man who is standing nearby the cock gives a starting signal, everyone race with shouts for first, second and third position. The cock is cooked with salt ginger and *rhusemialata* berries and are given eleven pieces to the first, nine to the second, and seven pieces to the third. These people are considered as the smartest men in the village. Before the cock is killed the eldest man holds it and invokes prayer. "This is going to sacrifice for this field, nine rivulets have been crossed, therefore, let there be no sickness, nine rivers have been crossed, so let there be no languor. He had paid the price for all those". He then strangles to cock to death and takes it to the jungle for cooking. As usual, a splendid feat is held in the midst of the day. In the evening before dusk, they will return home in queue with singing and war cry in enchanting tune.

In the second phase, he calls only the womenfolk to clean his field. This time no religious ceremony is performed. On the ninth day after the mithun sacrifice, he calls both men and women to work in his jhum field. Unlike any other day, on this day work become secondary and the feast become primary. The relatives and the in-laws of the giver will not work, instead they will drink the rice beer and cheer the common people by shouting "*Mami ghalo = in law come*", *Azi nonlo = group be happy, Nonthi, Nonlo = be joyful*". At night, a campfire with another feast is given where people of every age come to watch and enjoy the feast.

Feeding Fowls and Field Goers

The series of Feast of Merit end with feeding the villagers fowls and feeding the field goers. This is the supplementary ceremony to the Mithun Sacrifice. Seven or nine bamboo mats are laid in all the khels and the paddy spread on it challenging the whole villager's fowls to beak. The villagers will chase their fowls towards the paddy being spread in order to let them beak the paddy. In the evening when all the fowls go to the raft for a sleep the workers will gather remaining paddy and gave it to the poor people in village.

Again, an information is announced to all the villagers about the path feeding ceremony. The giver brews the rice beer sufficient to feed the whole villager. On the fixed day, a pig or cow is killed to eat with drinks. In the evening when the field goers are about to return home from the field, all the workers will divide the field path and carry the rice beer, cooked meat along with the leaf cups and plates to the outskirts of the village. Everyone who comes from the field will be heavily fed with drinks and meat. It is a facts that even, the enemy of the host (if he has) will partake the drinks and meat provided by the host. With this, the relation between them improves.

Notes and References

1. Common people used low or no verandah.
2. *The Ao Nagas* p. 257.
3. Verrier Elwin, *The Nagas in the 19th Century*, p. 217
4. The door is made up of split bamboos
5. It is the tradition of the Rengmas, every man keeps a special friend who made a covenant to help each other for the rest of life. They act as priests for each other especially in small religious ceremonies.
6. A handful of paddy put in small bambusa basket, and then sprinkled with water on it, till it germinates. The germinated paddy is dried and pounded in wooden mortar. The flour mixed with water in a gourd is called ajüxhi.
7. In most of the minor ceremonies bamboo knife is used.
8. It is believed that human being has nine spirits, and the nine twigs torn represent the human spirit. Three segments signify the father, mother and the child.
9. The upper layer is used for binding the top, the bottom segments, and the middle layer is used for binding the middle sigment.
10. The Mao Nagas bind clothes around the waist and over the shoulder on the warpath.
11. Seven pieces of lever is an offering to the Spirit God.
12. Exclusively used for religious purposes and considered it as the blessing treasury of God.
13. An Oral Interview with Mr. Kapo Apon of Sishunu Village on 5 Nov., 2001.
14. An Oral Interview with Mr. Hichulo Dukha of Kandinu Village on 20 Nov., 2001.
15. J.P. Mills, *The Rengma Nagas*, p. 190.
16. Signify the spear of the warrior
17. Honey-comb signify the good generation,
18. In 1997, at Sishunu village, in the cultural program I saw Mr. Kegwanye and his party killing a puppy alive by cutting it into two pieces

19. An Oral Interview with Manthi Kath of Kandinu Village on 30 Jan. 2001.
20. Manthi Kath of Kandinu Village killed 11 Cows and 9 Pigs.
21. See Page. 91
22. See Page. 85
23. See Page. 83
24. R.B. Dixon, *The Northern Maidu*, Bull. Am. Mus. National History XVII Part 3 1905, p. 328.
25. Verrier, *The Nagas in the 19th Century*, p. 474.
26. R. Brown, Narrative Report of the progress of the survey party, Naga Hills Season 1874, pp. 20-6.
27. An Oral Interview Report with Mr. Manthi, Mr. Shüghüphen and Mr. Sajukha Kath. All of them from Kandinu Village.
28. The Art and Crafts of Nagaland, Naga Institute of Culture, Government of Nagaland, Kohima 1968. p. 47.

Chapter 8

Fesitvals: Ngada or Akhu Festival

Ngada or Akhu is the Rengma Naga Festival, which is usually celebrated at the end of November, every year after the harvested grains had been brought to the village granary. It is one of the greatest festivals of the Rengma. It is a festival of feasting, dancing, singing, games, procession in colourful traditional dresses, rejoicing with friends, relations and even strangers. The main foods of the festival are pork, beef, and chicken curry and rice beer. Even the poorest man will kill a cock. The Akhu festival is not just feasting and merry making alone but it is a time of thanking the spirit God for the passed year blessings. As it is the main festival of the year, every villager eagerly waits for this season to celebrate. Akhu festival marks the end of the year, so preparation for the new cultivation begins as soon as Akhu celebration has ended.

Preliminary Ceremony of the Festival

According to the custom, Akhu can not start unless preliminary ceremonies are performed. As soon as all the villagers finished carrying the harvested grains from field to their respective granaries, the preparation of Akhu preliminary ceremonies begins. There are three preliminary ceremonies for the Akhu festival.[1]

1. Crab offering Genna

The first preliminary ceremony is called Crab Offering Genna. It is genna to save the harvested grains. Every household will go to the streams in search of female crabs for a burn offering to God. The next day early in the morning, mother or daughter (if mother is dead) goes to the family granary to perform ritual with crab rice and ash wrapped in *musa sumatrama* leaves. She makes the fire in front of the granary and then burns the crab wrapped along with rice and ash as an offering to the spirit God for abundance blessing upon the granary.[2] After propitiating God she comes back home and eats meal with the crabs' curry.

2. Paddy Top Layer Eating Genna

The second preliminary ceremony is called Paddy Top Layer Eating Genna. Here too, mother goes to the granary early in the morning, and takes a small handful of paddy from the top layer in the granary. On her way she will not speak to any one even if a person speaks to her. She pounds the paddy with a pestle and cooks it. After cooking, she eats it with crabs curry. Thenceforth family is free to take paddy for their daily need.

3. Jungle Clearance Ceremony

The third preliminary ceremony is called Jungle clearance genna. On this day, every man will test his luck for the New Year cultivation. Early in the morning a man (father) from every family goes to his would be field without speaking to anyone. There he clear little jungle and makes fire and then watches the smoke whether it goes up straight or in zigzag direction. It is believed that if the smoke goes up straight it is a sign of prosperity and good yielding for the year whereas zigzag direction will yield bad harvest of the year. On the same spot, he tests another omen. He cuts a stem of *moeselindica* and slices small pieces to the ground and observes its fall. If the fall is exactly as he expects, it is considered as a good sign of the harvest. Nevertheless, if it falls beyond his expectation, it is considered a sign of bad omen, so he may even abandon the side and shift to another plot for cultivation

Ngada or Akhu Festival

As soon as the above preliminary ceremonies were completed, preparation of the festival begins immediately. Now, every household will brew rice beer and arrange meat for the festival. As and when the preparation is over, the ceremonial Headman (senior most priest) will announce the date of Ngada or Akhu celebration in the evening. The next day, Akhu festival celebration begins which takes seven days to complete.

1. The first day is called rice beer making day. Everyone stays home and makes rice beer for the celebration.
2. The second day is called graves repairing and cleaning day. The graves of parents, ancestors and relatives are repaired and cleansed. Besides the village, surroundings were clean up. In order to appease the dead souls and to get more strength from them, they clean the graves.
3. The third day is called leaf cup placing day. Women of the village place leaf cups filled with rice beer on the graves of the dead. It is believed that ancestors

have the power to bring good harvest to their descendant. Therefore, they offer rice beer to the dead souls in order to please them.

4. The fourth day is called the day of bathing, washing clothes and weapons. Everyone goes to the village spring or wells and washes one's body, clothes and weapons in order to get rid of the passed impurities and to become new with the New Year. All the traditional dresses are taken out from cane basket (Japa or Allishon) and spread it in the sun heat, which beautifies the compound of the house. The traditional dress that is required to be repaired is done on this day.
5. The fifth day is called feasting day. Early in the morning the ceremonial headman goes to the village morung (Azüüqhuüü) and places rice beer (Azzütsa) by the foot of Totem pole (Aghon) which is an offering to the spirit God. A heavy feasting with in-laws, relatives, friends, and strangers'[3] from other village takes place before the procession starts. In the afternoon, male and female regardless of age will gather in front of morung (in certain villages khel to khel celebrate separately) with full dresses and ornaments. From there, they go for procession around the village with singing and dancing.
6. The sixth day is called young people dancing day. All the young people wear full dresses and ornaments and go round the whole village visiting house to house with singing songs and dancing. Moreover, in each house they are given beer to drink with meat. Thereafter, they gather at the morung and do merry making until late night.
7. The seventh day is called closing ceremony day. It is taboo to go to field on this day. Nevertheless, there is no restriction for other manual works at home or in

the jungle. On this day their traditional dresses are cleaned and kept in the same basket till the next Akhu festival or some time are used on some important occasion.

In this way, the Rengma Nagas celebrate Akhu festival. The next day onward, every one becomes busy for clearing the jungle for cultivation.[4]

Notes

1. Tour Diary of Lieutenant Bigges, Assistant Agent, detached to the Naga Hills to Captain Jenkins, Agent Governor-General. N.E Frontier Communicated from the political secretariat of India to the secretary to the Asiatic Society, 1841. J.A.S.B. Vol. X Part 1, pp. 129-36.
2. Female crab is used because it has hundreds of eggs.
4. Tour Diary of Captain A.E. Woods, I.S.C., Deputy Commissioner of the Naga Hills, for the month of February 1894.
4. Speech delivered by Mr. Nillo Rengma at Akhu festival celebration on 28th November 2002 at Rengmapani village.

Chapter 9

Folk Tales

Brothers Trap Birds

One day two brothers went to trap the birds. They could snare a good number of birds. On their way back home, unfortunately, they lost their way, and, to their surprise, they entered the tiger's den. The tiger felt happy and told the two brothers, "For the passed few days I did not get my food, but now you have come, so I am going to eat you." Elder brother replied, "Uncle tiger, we have plenty of birds sufficient for your hunger. Eat these birds, and allow us to go home." Then said, the tiger, "feed me". The elder brother made the fire, and started roasting the birds to feed the tiger. Meanwhile without having any intention, the younger brother dug the earth to make the hearth for the tiger. Fortunately, he found the granite. When a single bird was left, he told the tiger that the bird was about to finish. The tiger replied, after finishing the birds I would devour both of you. Knowing the attitude of the tiger, the younger brother put the granite in the fire. The elder brother then, requested the tiger to wait for some time for the last piece. When the granite became hot, he asked the tiger to close his eyes and open his mouth to receive the last piece. The tiger obeyed his instruction. He immediately put the hot granite into the tiger's mouth. The inflicted tiger lay there groaning, with no one to help him. Taken the advantage of their adversary's pain the two brothers asked the tiger to go out from the den for the waterfall and escape from the jaw of death. The tiger ran out in a great speed for the water. The tiger opened his jaw wide and let the cool waterfall into his throat. While she was doing so, a small bird (Hiphiwa) brown in colour flew into the mouth of the tiger and came out from its anus. But when the bird was almost at the anus, the tiger closed its anus and tied up the tail of the bird. Helpless bird left his tail in the anus of the tiger and flew away from the tiger. This bird (Hiphiwa) does not have its tail, and is forbidden to eat it by the Rengma.

How Day and Night Came into Being

Once upon a time all the living creatures on the earth held a meeting to choose their leader. An owl happens to be very handsome with slender body and, somewhat pointed head and beautiful eyes. Hence, they chose him to be their king. When he became the king, he ordered the universe to remain day for nine years at a stretch and then to become night for nine years at a stretch. It resulted an untold misery to the living creatures. In this, regard all the living creatures came to the king and beat him on his head. In consequence upon his miss-rule, his head and body became short and flat with bulging eyes.

The general body held another meeting and decided to choose a new king. They chose wren to be their king. Wren (Songbird) through singing ordered the universe to remain half-day and half-night in a day, which enabled the creatures to work and sleep respectively. The happiness of the creatures knew no bound, so they all came and rubbed their ruler gently. Due to their gentle touch wren became smaller and smaller as we can see even this day.

Poaching of the Baby Bird

One day two brothers went in search of the chicks in the thick of the jungle. There they found three chicks in its nest on one of the large trees. They climbed up the tree by nailing wood splinters as a ladder. Both of them wanted to have the oldest chick, but the younger brother took it. The elder brother felt bad on the matter and decided to give up the programme of taming the bird. He left his younger brother on the tree and climbed down. As he climbed down all the wood was removed which was used as a ladder. The younger brother has no alternative to come down; he stayed there with the chicks.

When the parents of the chicks brought food for their little ones, they saw young boy sitting with their chicks. The parents inquired the boy, why he is there with their chicks. He replied, an evil man came here to take away your children, so I am here guarding them. The parents of the chicks were delighted. And out of their joy, they used to steal the food of the farmers in the field and feed the young boy. On the other side, he used to pluck out the wing-feathers and the tails of the chicks lest they fly away. After several days, the parents of the chicks told the boy; it is time for them to fly with us and requested the boy not to pluck their chicks' feathers any more. Poor boy replied, if they fly away I have no other means for living. The parents felt pity on the boy and told him, "we will bring a strong wind to push down the tree on the ground and allow you to get down." Within a few days it happened and enabled the young boy to go home.

It so happen that by the time he reached home it was late night; he knocked at the door, and requested his mother to open the door. The mother denied, thinking that her son might have died long day's back. At last, he said, "Mother, if you do not believe your son, please give me bamboo mat, which I was knitting before I left this house with my elder brother". The mother gave him the mat, but did not allow him to sleep inside the house. The sad boy rolled the mat and then sleeps inside it. Unfortunately, mosquitoes sucked all his blood and he died of it on that night. The next morning the mother saw her son lying dead. She could not do anything but mourned and regretted for her guilt.

The Flower and the Girl Friend

In a certain village, there lived a handsome boy and a beautiful girl, who had deep love affair. There relation became more than the husband and wife. Whatever one does it was for the sack of the other. There was nothing that could depart them from each other. Their relation was knitted like the fishing net. One day they went to the jungle to collect the firewood, suddenly the girl saw a beautiful flower blooming at the top of the tree. Her desire to get the flower entailed her to request the boy to pluck the flower. Without doubt and fear he gave a positive response to his lover. Before he could reach the flower, to his wonder, the tree grew taller and taller. He could neither pluck nor come down. Jump from the tree was the last option. So he shouted to his lover to spread her skirt on the ground. In her terror and puzzle, she somehow spread her skirt as requested by her beloved lover. However, her lover's body could reach the ground in small pieces. Only his thigh and toe could reach the skirt, the rest of the flesh spread on the ground. Nothing, but her desire to have the natural beauty brought to an end the unbroken relation.

Owl's Food

In the beginning, God created the living creatures. He also made their food for living. He than asked them to choose their own food. Accordingly, every living creature chose his or her own food. So did the owl. She chooses the deciduous tree (Ammishü), whose fruit is green in colour but will never ripe. By the time they choose their own food, this particular tree (Ammishü-tong) was having its fruits abundantly with green juicy colour. The owl was happy and thought that the fruits of the tree she had chosen would be delicious and sufficient for her life. At that time no other tree was bearing any fruit, therefore, she thought that she was the wisest and luckiest among her friends. She flew to ammishü-tong, and was patiently waiting for the fruits to get ripe. While she was waiting, all the other trees started bearing its fruits and began to ripen for their dependence. All the birds started enjoying their fruits: yet, an unfortunate owl waits and waits until the last fruit of the tree fed away.

Trapping the Bird

Through out the dry season a father and his son trapped the birds in their field. They used to send home some birds for the mother. The mother too, sends the food items to them through third person. Through the carrier, she sent an instruction to husband and son; that, they should eat food separately and should not see each other's food. They strictly maintained the instruction of the mother.

One day a quail sang near their field. The boy responded to the bird by saying, "Though you sing sweetly; your chest muscle meat is sour." On hearing it his father asked, what is the taste of the muscle? It is sour, replied the son. No, it is very tasty, said the father. The son said, my mother used to send me cooked chest muscle everyday, which tastes so sour. Then the father checked the son's food and found Abonthi (Elephant fruit), which is rough and sour. He came to realize that his wife is not in good terms with his son. Hence, they have decided not to send the bird any more. The wife was not happy, and made a plan to raid to snare birds. She plaited her hair, placed it at the top of her head, and then proceeded toward the field. When she reached their fields, she shouted to her husband and son, saying enemies from the Angami region is coming to attack you, you should run for your life. The two trappers thought that it is true, and escaped to the jungle. She swiftly collected the birds from the noose and left for home.

The Bumblebee

Mr. Thsütsalibvü and Miss. Sunthu were in love with each other, the two lovebirds could have no other plan but to unite in marriage and live the rest of life in love and happiness. The boy was from a poor family whereas the girl was from a relatively richer family. Their proposal for marriage was turned down by the girl's parents. It's parent's prerogative to arrange a groom for her. So she can't marry the man she loves. She was forced to marry another man from the well to do family who was from a far distance village. Several years later Thsütsalinvü became a great warrior and popular to his village.

One day he went to his former girl friend's village for some business, and then paid a casual visit to her. She offered him the rice beer, and they had some discussion, which let to a lengthy conversation. On the other hand, her husband, who was jealous of the great warrior, ordered the villagers to fence nine times round the village, to keep the warrior from fleeing. Seeing her husband sharpening his dao and spear, she could sense the unusual behavior of her husband. She therefore, signals the man to run for life by kicking his cup. However, Thsütsalibvü did not realize the danger to his life. At last, she catches one of the chicks and strangles its head to death, and then puts it inside the cup of the guest. The warrior realized the danger and ran out of the village. He could successfully jump over the nine fences, but his warrior-shawl (allon-thsü) hung in one of the poles. With the shawl in his hand, his enemy shouted at him; "How could a warrior and the chief of the village left his shawl in this manner? Shy: That fellow warrior is as timid as the dog. How will he meet his villager without his king-shawl? Oh! Shame! He is not worth to claim a warrior." The infuriated man could not withstand the insulting statements, so he skipped back to take his shawl; but his enemy speared him to death.

The enemy cut his penis and took it. Whereas his villagers carried his corpse home for burial. He (the killer of the man) always places the penis nearby his wife's working place. She was peeved and complained to her husband, but he simply mocked her. Therefore, she took her beloved penis, dried it, and then ground it into powder. She made yeast out of it and put it in the rice beer. She made her husband drink. As soon as the cup was finished he fell and died. The dead body was wrapped with the cloths and ran for original home. She mourned three days and nights on her lover's grave without food and drink. On the third day, she transformed into Bumblebee.

There came out another Bumblebee from the grave and they flew away happily. It is therefore, believed that those two lovers had turned into bumblebee. Even now, especially in the spring season, we notice two gay bumblebees fully hovering over our head at home, and some times in our jhum field.

Two Orphans

In a village, a family consists of parents, one son, and a daughter poor. It was unfortunate for the two children to live without their parents. While they were young they had lost both of their parents by dead, and caused them to be orphans. They have no relatives to look after them; as such their living condition was miserable. One day, gentleman from the other village came to their village. He met the poor orphan lady and fall in love with her. He therefore, decided to marry her. The lady too, could not resist the attraction of the young man; hence, true love began to bloom in their hearts. They joined hands to live together for the rest of their life. With the departure of the lady for her new home, the poor unfortunate boy was left at the mercy of the villagers. Taking the advantage of the innocent boy, one of the villagers sold him to another village as a baby-sitter. The buyer in his term sold him to another village, as it was the system prevailed in the past. In the same way he was sold to nine different villages. Through out the transactions he was sold as the baby-sitter.

Fortunately or un-fortunately, at the ninth village, the housewife seemed to be so cruel. He was treated beyond the measure of the slave. During his rest time he was forced to carry a whetstone. The process of life was so hard for the boy to proceed further. One day, out of pain and sorrow his memory call the childhood life at will, and then, carrying the baby at his back started singing lullaby with the words, "Oh my father Okha, my mother Nella and my sister Mashule! Why have you left me alone in this miserable world? I wish to live with you like the bygone days. Are there any more places for us to live together again? ...I am tired of this life." By hearing the boy singing melancholy lullaby, the baby's mother asked the boy to repeat the song. On hearing her parent's name and her name called by the boy through song, she was impressed. Thereafter, she started checking the boy's cap, and found a scar on his head. She inquisitively asked him, why a scar on your head? He replied, "While I was warping with my sister, I miss-handled the thread-ball and it slipped out of my hand. My sister got angry and stroked my head with her shuttle. She came to realize that the baby-sitter is no other than her own brother. She cut his hair and allowed him to take bath, thereafter, changed his rag cloths with the new cloths. In the evening when her husband came back from the field, he saw the boy so fresh and smart. So he sarcastically said, "Servant is different today." But she told her husband that their servant is her own brother. And explained the matter in detail to her husband. Thenceforward, they lived happily.

Few years later, she requested her brother to go back home. She said, "Brother, we are living in a foreign land where we do not have any legal right on anything. You have got our ancestor's properties in our native land. Therefore, it will be good if you go home." On the day of leaving for his native place, his sister prepared a heavy load of presents, such as dao, sword, mithun etc. and told him not to use the sword on his way. It so happened that on his way *bambusa* branch got hold of his basket. To clear the way he cut the *bambusa* with the dao, but it did not help him much so he used the sword to cut it. Though he could clear the way, he cut his knee while cutting the *bambusa* with the sharp sword. He succumbed to his injury on the spot. Had he obey the instruction of his sister he would have escaped from the mouth of death. After nine days, a crow came and crowed on the roof of her house. "Today is the ninth day of your brother's death". Instantly she went in search of him. Except, the tail, the whole body of the mithun was found petrified. She collected the tail of the mithun and carried the decomposed body of her brother to the village for burial. The petrified stone is still seen on the incident spot in Rengma area.

The Cicada

In the mid-summer a mother with her child and a baby-sitter went to her jhum field. She kept the child under the care of the baby-sitter and left for weeding the field. The field is over-grown with weeds, so she was busy with the work and was not much concerned to feed her crying child. Even the lunchtime was passed, but she didn't come, so the baby-sitter called her mummy to come for the lunch. Both of them were hungry and tired, hence, she shouted to her mummy, if you do not turn up now I am going to change into a cicada. The mother replied, "wait for a while", but didn't come on time. Then, she bound herself with the lullaby shawl and held the post of the hut. Instantly, she was changed into a cicada and began to sing pleasantly. When the mother came for the lunch, she saw the cicada singing sweetly on the roof of the hut was no other than the baby-sitter. The mother looked at the cicada in astonishment, and requested to re-incarnate. But it was unfortunate that it no longer understood the language. She tried to catch the insect, but it flew away and did not return again. The mother knew that it will not return, yet, out of pain and sad she prepared her food and lay on the raft of the hut. Next day, when she went back to her field, she saw the food laid for the cicada was turned into mushroom.

Lizard and Thrush

On one occasion, a lizard and a thrust decided to lay their eggs at one place; as their eggs are similar. Both of them laid as much as they could and when the egging season was over, they decided to share their eggs equally. While doing so, one egg was found in excess. Both of them wanted to take the extra one. In a way, miss-understanding was aroused between them. Eventually, an agreement was reached: that they will fight and who ever wins shall take the excess egg.

Both of them arranged fans and supporters. A lizard brought all the animals that crawl on the earth while the thrush brought all the fowls that fly in the sky. A phalanger too, was present. All the members of both families were present on that auspicious day. The python among the crawlers who won the applause of the spectators initiated a spectacular game. Python stood up and challenged the fowls. When the python called for the duel, all the opponents were aghast. They had no nerve to fight. Everyone winked at each other and asked each other to go for the duel. The arena was filled with only the murmuring noise of the fowls. However, one of the fowls that was sitting in the corner observing the great commotion stood up and said, "I can". The fowl was no other than the mighty 'Eagle'. Suddenly the commotion died down at once, and in the arena remained a pin drop silence for a while. Again, the spectators gave a loud applause.

After complying with all the formalities, they tangled by applying their best tactics. When the python fell, all the fowls applauded loudly whereas the crawlers wept. Moreover, when the eagle falls, all the crawlers applauded loudly whereas the fowls wept. Yet, the tricky phalanger always stood at the winning side. In the long fight python was defeated, and the eagle trod on the python with its claws and then slowly lifted it up to the tree. The happiness of the fowls knew no bound whereas the crawlers wept bitterly. Interestingly, both teams refused to include phalanger in their group for being flexible, and left alone to her own destiny. Even to this day the phalanger hides inside the hollow tree and come out at dawn.

The eagle requested the eldest among the fowls to come for cutting the python. Aqoqu (Woodpecker genus) considered herself the eldest walked forward and cut the snake with its beak. She paints her body in various colours with the blood of the python. Thereafter all the fowls paint their respective body with the python blood and become beautiful at their own choice. The dove was the last bird to come on the next morning. There was nothing left, except tiny moral pasted on the wood. She painted her legs with it and flew away. For this reason, people believed that the different colours of every fowl was painted from the blood of the python, killed by the eagle

Liar Boy

A boy was considered the worst liar in the village. His friends felt strong indignation against him. Many a time his parents used to hear the report without any evidence. Therefore, one day his father took him to the field in order to prove rumours. Though there was no deer, he suddenly cried out and said, "Son, there is a deer standing near the field". Then his son responded to him "Oh! Yes, there are two deer standing". As soon as he proved the truth of his son's lies, he punished his son. He bound his son at a tree, and fenced nine times round the son. The son was kept for an over-night. At night a tiger came, pulled down all the fences and devoured the poor liar boy.

Village Without Fundament

Once upon a time, a tricky fellow always played pranks on people. His name was Aki. He went to a village where none of the villager had a fundament. He saw the villagers inhaling the odour of the food and water, and then throwing it away when it lost its aroma. They neither ate nor drank, because they did not have a hole to pass the excreta. In the presence of the public he ate the food and drank the wine. Then, climbing up a lane tree passed out the excretion. The villagers were amazed and asked him how this could be done. Aki told them that he made a hole at his anus, through which he could release the excreta. The excited parents requested him to do the same to their sons. Though, outwardly he accepted their request reluctantly, yet, he wished to perform in his heart. Before he began his operation, villagers offered him a splendid feast. He asked the villagers to arrange a large bamboo basket. All the villagers brought their children to Aki. He put all the children in the basket, poked their fundament with hot iron rod, and then closed it. He told the villagers not to open until he reaches the hill top near the village and shouted to them. Accordingly they opened the basket and found not a single child was alive. They got wild and chased him with dao and spear. Aki got tired so he climbed up a tree and hid there. When the villagers reached the same place, they too felt tired and rested under the tree where Aki was hiding. One of the youths got very angry for not being able to chaste Aki, therefore, he cut the same tree by saying, "If Aki is standing near-by I will kill him like this". Out of fear, he urinated on the head of his hunters. However, the chasers thought it as raining and went back home. Aki was luckily saved.

Miss Allu and the Tiger

Once upon a time, there lived Mr. Khakkhu with his pregnant wife in a very remote village. One day, she told her husband that she wanted to eat the fig fruit. Without any objection, he went to the jungle to pluck fruits for his wife. He kept his bambusa basket near the tree and climbed up to pluck the fruits. While he was plucking the fruits a tiger came and said, this basket belongs to Mr. Khakkhu, where is he? If I meet him, I will eat him". By hearing the deadly words from the tiger, Khakkhu could not keep mum. He replied, our wife is pregnant now, and she wants to eat this fig fruit so I am here collecting for her. The tiger responded, you have said, she is our wife therefore, when she deliver a child you should give it to me, if not I will eat you now. Khakkhu sadly agreed.

After the incident, the tiger regularly inquired weather a child is delivered. Khakkhu lied to the tiger, although the child was already born some months back. He named her as Allu, which means my beloved. When the tiger complained that the pregnancy will not last such a long period, he told the truth. Though Allu is already grown up, yet he lied to the tiger this time too, by telling the tiger that the child is still sucking her mother's breast. Khakkhu could no longer control his emotion. So when his daughter saw tears rolling on his cheeks, she asked the reason for crying. Then he replied that while cutting the bamboo he had got injured.

A day was fixed to hand over his daughter to the tiger. He told the tiger to wait at the edge of their field near-by the Athsütsa-thighi(a genus of orchid). On the fixed day they went to their field and asked his daughter to pluck the flower at the edge of the field. When she went to pluck the flower, the tiger caught her. From that day onward she became the wife of the tiger. But she did not stop crying. Therefore, the tiger brought dolls, eatable things to pacify her cry but that too could not subside her lamentation.

One day she told the tiger that she was going to prepare rice beer for him and requested him to go to field alone. The tiger went to the field alone. When the tiger was about to reach home she torched their house and went to her parent's house. As and when the tiger came and saw their house burning the tiger asked Allu's parents where their daughter Allu is? They replied that they saw Allu burning in the fire.

Instantly, the tiger jumped into the fire by saying "I will burn myself with Allu". From that time onward Allu could re-join her parents and lived happily with them.

References

Bareh, H., *Gazetteer of India Nagaland Kohima District* printed by S.N. Guha Ray at Sree Saraswatty Press Ltd, 32, Acharya Prafulla Chandra Road, Calcutta, 9. May 1970.

Bordoloi, B.N. and Sharma Thakur, *Tribes of Assam* Part II, T.R.I Popular Series. Tribal Research Institute, Assam, Guwahati, First Edition, 1988.

Butler John, *Travels in Assam*, Mamas Publication Delhi. 1994.

Census of India 1981, Series 15 Nagaland Part XC Survey Report on village Tseminyu. Publish by the controller of publications, Civil Lines, Delhi.

Elwin Varrier, *The Nagas in the Nineteenth Century*, Oxford University Press, Ely House, London W.I Oxford House, Apollo Bunder, Bombay IBR, 1969.

– –, *India's North-East Frontiers in the Nineteenth Century*, Oxford University Press, Ely House, London W.I Oxford House, Madras, Third Impression, 1972.

Folk Tales from Nagaland, Directorate of Art and Culture Government of Nagaland, Kohima. First Published 1971, Second Enlarged Edition 1989.

G.K. Ghosh, *Tribals and their Culture, Manipur and Nagaland,*, Vol. 3.

Ganguli Milada, *A Pilgrimage to the Nagas*, Mohan Primlani for Oxford & IBH Publishing Co., New Delhi, 1984.

Gazetteer of India, Nagaland, Kohima District. Printed by S.N. Guha Ray at Sree Saraswatty Press Ltd., 32, Acharya Prafulla Chandra Road, Calcutta, May 1970.

George E.R., *Extracts from the Journal of an expedition into the Naga Hills, J.A.S.B.*, 1840, Vol. IX Part II, pp. 947-53.

Ghosh, B.B., *Nagaland District Gazetteers Tuensang District, Government of Nagaland Kohima 1981*, printed at Sethi Printers Dimapur, Nagaland. The Ao Nagas.

Hastings James, *Encyclopaedia of Religion and Ethics*, Vol XI., Edinburg: T & T - Clark, 38 George Street New York: Charles Scribner's Sons, 597. Fifth Avenue. Sixth Impression, 1967.

Hutton, J.H., *Tour Diary of the Deputy Commissioner*, Naga Hills for the year 1926. Political-B. June 1927. Nos. 707-737.

— —, *The Angami Nagas*, Published by Macmillan and Co. Limited, London 1921. Second edition by Oxford University Press 1961.

— —, *The Sema Nagas*, Published by Macmillian & Co. Limited, London, 1921. Second edition; Directorate of Art and Culture, Government of Nagaland, 1968.

Kumar B.B., *Journal of Social Research* Special Number on Nagaland, Published by the Council of Social and Cultural Research Bihar and the Department of Anthropology, Ranchi University, Ranchi Vol. XXVII 1984.

Mills J.P., *The Lotha Nagas*, Published by Macmillian & Co. Limited, London, 1922. Second edition; Directorate of Art and Culture, Government of Nagaland, 1980.

— —, *The Rengma Nagas*, Published by Macmillian & Co. Limited, London, 1937. Second edition; Directorate of Art and Culture, Government of Nagaland, 1982.

— —, Published by Directorate of the Government of Nagaland, Oxford University Press Calcutta, 1973.

Paxton John, *The New Illustrated Everyman's Encyclopaedia*, Octupus Book Limited 59, Grossvenor Street, London W.I Vol. 1 First edition 1984.

Report on the Administration of the Naga Hills, No. 112T, dated Shillong, the 17th May 1872. From Colonel. H. Hopkinson, Agent to

Governor General North East Frontier, and Commissioner of Assam Judl. Department.

Robinson William, *A Descriptive Account of Assam,* 1841.

The Arts and Crafts of Nagaland, Naga Institute of Culture Government of Nagaland, Kohima; Published by Shri. M. Alemchiba Ao on behalf of the Naga Institute of Culture, Government of Nagaland. July 1968.

The New Encyclopaedia Britannica in 30 Volumes. Vol I, Founded 1768, 15th Edition. Encyclopaedia Britannica, Inc, William Benton, Publisher 1943-1973. Helen Hemingway Benton, Publisher, 1973-1974, London/Chicago Etc.

Tour Dairy of Captain W.M. Kennedy, I.S.C., offg. Deputy Commissioner Naga Hills for the month of July 1901.

Tour Dairy of Deputy Commissioner, Naga Hills for 1937. Governor's Secretariat, Appointment and Political Department. File No. GS/280.

Tour Diary of C.R. Pawsay, ESQMC, I.C.S., Deputy Commissioner, Naga Hills 1920 -1947.

Tour Diary of Captain A.E. Woods, I.S.C., Deputy Commissioner of the Naga Hills for the month of February 1894. A.S.P.O. (Judl.) No. 517-40-31-3-94.

Tour Diary of Captain H.W.G. Cole, I.S.C., Deputy Commissioner of the Naga Hills for the Month of Oct'1897 Political Department.

Watterrs Thomas, *On Chwang's Travels in India* (AD 625-65) London 1904. Delhi Reprint 1973.

Woods Lt. A.E., Assistant Commissioner Naga Hills, I.S.C. No. 24, Dated 8-5-1892.

Interviews

1. Manthi Kath of Kandinu village. He had hosted the Real Feast of Merit (Githie) Ceremony.
2. Shughupen Wanth of Kandinu village. He had hosted the Real Feast of Merit (Githie) Ceremony

3. Chenga Semy of Nsunyu village. He had hosted the Real Feast of Merit (Githie) Ceremony. He has recently converted to Christianity.
4. Nonzawa Kez of Tesophenyu village. He had hosted the Real Feast of Merit (Githie). He still professes the traditional religion.
5. Hichulo Dukha of Kandinu village. He had acted as the helper of the priest in the religious ceremonies.
6. Khetu Kath of Kandinu Village. He had acted as the helper of the priest in the religious ceremonies.
7. Kethang Kath of Kandinu Village. He had acted as the helper of the priest in the religious ceremonies.

Index